London
Great Britain

This guide offers a selection of London's hotels, restaurants and stores hand-picked from the thousands the city has to offer.

KNOPF
CITY GUIDES

2

3

5

5

6

**THIS IS A BORZOI BOOK
PUBLISHED BY
ALFRED A. KNOPF, INC**

Copyright © 1998 Alfred A.
Knopf Inc., New York

ISBN 0-375-70255-5

Library of Congress number

97-80568

First published May 1998

Originally published in
France by Nouveaux Loisirs,
a subsidiary of Gallimard,
Paris 1997, and in Italy by
Touring Editore, Srl.,
Milano 1997.
Copyright © 1997
Nouveaux Loisirs,
Touring Editore, Srl.

SERIES EDITORS
EDITORIAL MANAGER:
Seymourina Cruse
LONDON EDITION :
Seymourina Cruse
with Caroline Cuny
GRAPHICS
Élizabeth Cohat, Yann Le Duc
LAYOUT:
Olivier Lauga, Yann Le Duc
MINI-MAPS, AIRPORT MAPS:
Kristoff Chemineau
AROUND LONDON MAPS:
Édigraphie
STREET MAPS:
Touring Club Italiano
PRODUCTION
Catherine Bourrabier

Translated by Yvonne Worth

Edited and typeset by Book
Creation Services, London

Printed in Italy by
Editoriale Libraria

Authors and editors
LONDON

Things you need to know:
Seymourina Cruse (1)
Author of various guides for *The Best of
Lyon*, Le Petit Paumé, Gallimard, Eurostar,
Havas and the magazine *Grands Reportages*,
Seymourina travels extensively and visits
London regularly.

Where to stay:
Mary-Anne Evans (2)
Coordinator of numerous works on hotels
and restaurants of London, Mary-Anne
helped compile Gault Millau's guide, *The
Best of London*; a magazine published by
British Heritage, and the American
magazine *Gourmet*. She is also in charge of
the monthly publication *Where London*.

Where to eat: Guy Dimond (3)
Contributor to the restaurants sections of
Time Out, *Marie-Claire*, the *Good Food Guide*,
BBC Vegetarian Good Food and *Gourmet Good
Food*; Guy visits around 140 restaurants
each year. He has been nominated as a
finalist in the Glenfiddich Awards, the annual
award for best UK food critic.

After dark: Juliet Pospielovsky (4)
Responsible for the *Entertainment* section
(theatres, operas, concerts, jazz venues) for
the magazine *Where London*, Juliet was a
Latin-American dancer and an actress with
Rope Theatre.

What to see and Further
afield: Sarah McAlister (5)
Journalist for various Time Out guides and
the Rough Guide, Sarah has participated in
putting together numerous works on
London. As a professional tourist guide, she
regularly organized guided tours and visits
in and around London.

Where to shop: Jonathan Cox (6)
Journalist for *Time Out* magazine, Jonathan
has contributed to various editions of the
specialized publication *Shopping & Services
in London*, as well as writing several chapters
for Time Out and Dorling Kindersley guides.

How to use this guide

This guide is divided into eight separate sections: **Things you need to know** (information on travel and living in London); **Where to stay** (hotels); **Where to eat** (restaurants); **After dark** (going out); **What to see** (museums and monuments in the city); **Further afield** (places to visit around London); **Where to shop** (store guide); **Maps** (street maps and plan of the underground).

The **color** of the arrow box matches that of the corresponding dots on the mini-maps.

In the area gives you a feel for the location.

In the area
The South Bank Arts Centre – containin several Aroma sandwich bars – and Wat

The **area** (or the subject on a thematic page) is shown just above the map. A map reference allows you to find place easily in the street map section.

Waterloo   **F** 3B - 4B - 4C

⊖ *Temple*

In the area
The South Bank Arts Centre – containing The People's Palace and several Aroma sandwich bars – and Waterloo Station dominate this area. A short walk east along the bank of the Thames takes you to Gabriel's Wharf – a craft market with several inexpensive brasseries – to the

■ After dark → 88
■ What to see → 108

Impressive Oxo Tower

Where to eat

The People's Palace (87)
Royal Festival Hall, 4th floor, South Bank Centre, SE1
⊖ Waterloo, Embankment ☎ 0171-928 9999 ● 0171-928 2355
Modern British cuisine ●●● daily noon-
11pm, 5.30-11pm

The Royal Festival Hall is an impressive piece of 1950s architecture. The river-facing restaurant on Level 3 was given a new lease of life in 1995 with complete refurbishment. And its management, a team of staff who can handle everything from a well-done management, a team of staff who can Modern British cooking which is completely up-to-date with salmon and salsa verde or oven-pumpkin with camembell cream. Ask for a riverside seat: the views over the Thames are magnificent.

Oxo Tower Restaurant & Brasserie (88)
Barge House Street, South Bank, SE1
⊖ Blackfriars, Waterloo Modern British cuisine ☎ 0171-803 3888 ●●● Restaurant ●●●●
Mon.-Sat noon-3pm, 6-11pm; Sun. 11am-10pm ●● daily 11am-11pm; Sun.
11am-10pm ☎ 0171-803 3838

This landmark, used to be the world headquarters of a brand of stock cube, but was left empty for many years, until 1996 it was respected by Harvey Nichols for its brasserie and a more elegant and more expensive restaurant on the floor also, whose stunning is better value for money than the restaurant itself a bar. The range impressive enough, but these are also terrace and with stylish services and with stylish cooking. Reservations recommended for both luncheon and evening.

Livebait (89)
43 The Cut, SE1 ☎ 0171-928 7211
⊖ Waterloo Fish and seafood ●● Mon.-Sat noon-3pm, 5.30-11.30pm

This delightful restaurant is a short walk from Waterloo Station, and it is situated close to the Old Vic and Young Vic theaters it was once a Victorian pie and mash shop, and the look retains this heritage has been carefully restored displayed on an ice counter. The dried walk. Fresh fish and shellfish are the dishes are cooked to perfection quality of the fish and seafood is superb. particularly recommended, the staff friendly, and the prices are competitive.

Not forgetting
■ **The Fire Station (90)** 150 Waterloo Road, SE1 ☎ 0171-620 2226 ●●
Lively, noisy bar-restaurant is made up of primarily Modern British dishes. A good place to go for a quick drink before catching a train.

■ *Blackfriars, Waterloo **Modern British cuisin***
Mon.–Sat noon–3pm, 6–11pm; Sun. 11am–10p
11am–11pm; Sun. 11am–10pm ☎ *daily 11ar*

Not forgetting lists places we also recommend, but don't have space to cover in full here.

Not forgetting
■ **The Fire Station**
Lively, noisy bar-restaurant is made up of primarily M

Key information tells you what you ne to know about each particular place: the nearest underground station: the price rang accepted means of payment, and the variou services and facilities on offer.

The **opening page** of each section gives an index of its contents and some helpful hints.

Things you need to know contains information on getting to London and on travel and daily life in the city.

Thematic pages pick out a selection of establishments linked by a common element. These are also shown on a simplified map.

Detailed **maps** are given in the eighth section of the guide: a map of the subway and nine street maps.

Key

☎	telephone
➠	fax
●	price or price range
⊙	opening hours
▭	credit cards accepted
▣	credit cards not accepted
▼	toll-free number
@	e-mail address

Access

⊖	underground stations
P	parking
🏠	private parking
♿	facilities for the disabled
🚫	no facilities for the disabled
➲	train
🚗	car
⛵	boat
🚌	bus

Hotels

☏	telephone in room
🖷	fax in room on request
🍸	minibar
📺	television in room
Ⅲ	air-conditioned rooms
①	24-hour room service
💼	caretaker
🧒	babysitting
➕	meeting room(s)
🚫	no pets
☕	breakfast
🍵	open for tea/coffee
🍴	restaurant
🎵	live music
◎	discotheque
🌱	garden, patio or terrace
🏋	gym, fitness club
🏊	swimming pool, sauna

Restaurants

🥗	vegetarian food
🏔	view
👔	smart dress required
🚬	smoking area
🍸	bar

Museums and galleries

⊞	on-site store(s)
📕	guided tours
☕	café

Stores

🏪	branches, outlets

Time difference
London is 5 to 6 hours ahead of New York time and 8 to 9 hours ahead of San Francisco time.

Getting there

Pets
Britain is completely free of rabies and therefore has extremely strict regulations on bringing animals into the country. All animals entering the UK must, without exception, undergo a period of six months quarantine.

Electricity
Britain operates a 240-volt system and electrical items use three-prong plugs. Remember to bring an adaptor.

Average temperatures

The average temperature in London in July/August is 22°C (75°F), falling to 7°C (44°F) in December/January.

51 Things you need to Know

Passports

Visitors carrying a valid EU passport are entitled to unlimited entry to the UK; Europeans traveling with a national identity card are entitled to stay for six months. Children must have a passport or parental authorisation. Visitors from outside Europe must carry a valid passport.

Health

European visitors should bring with them form E111 in case of medical emergencies ➡ 15. Visitors from outside Europe should arrange health insurance cover before traveling.

Cars

In Britain vehicles drive on the left. To rent a car in the UK you will need a full internationally-valid driving license. If bringing your own vehicle into the country, always carry your insurance policy with you.

Basic facts

London has four international airports: **Heathrow**, 15 miles west of London; **Gatwick**, 28 miles south of London; **Stansted**, 40 miles north of London; and **City Airport** (internal and European flights), 7 miles east of central London. Airport taxi stands operate 24 hours a day.

Getting there

Heathrow

Information
☎ 0181-759 4321
Terminal 1
☎ 0181-745 7487
Terminal 2
☎ 0181-745 5408
Terminal 3
☎ 0181-745 4655
Terminal 4
☎ 0181-745 7302
Subway
Piccadilly line to Earl's Court (40 mins), Green Park (45 mins), Covent Garden (50 mins).
Bus
National Express direct to Victoria Coach Station (35 mins) ● £5.25
Airbus A1 to Victoria via Cromwell Road, Knightsbridge and Hyde Park

Corner (journey 1 hr), departures every 30 mins from 3.15am to 8.30pm ● £6
Airbus A2 to King's Cross via Bayswater Road, Marble Arch, Baker Street, Euston and Russell Square (1 hr 15 mins), departing every 30 mins, 5am to 9pm ● £6
Car rental
Avis
☎ 0181-899 1000
Hertz
☎ 0181-897 2072
Hotel
Heathrow Marriott
Ditton Road, Langley, Slough, Bucks SL3 8PT
☎ (01753) 544244
➡ (01753) 540272

Gatwick

Information
☎ (01293) 535353
Train
Gatwick Rail Express to Victoria Station (30 mins) ● £8.90
Bus
Flightline 777 direct to Victoria Coach Station (70 mins) ● £7.50
Car rental
Avis
☎ (01293) 529721
Hertz
☎ (01293) 530555
Hotel
Forte Crest
North Terminal, Gatwick Airport, West Sussex RH6 0PH
☎ (01293) 567070
➡ (01293) 567739

Stansted

Information
☎ (01279) 680500
Train
Stansted Express to Liverpool Street Station (40 mins) ● £10.40 (change at Tottenham Hale for the subway).
Bus
Flightline 777 direct to Victoria Coach Station (1 hr 25 mins) ● £9

Airport Transfer Ltd
☎ 0171-403 2228
Offers a pick-up service to take you from or drop you back at the airport. From London (W1) to Heathrow ● £18; Gatwick ● £35; Stansted ● £40 (add an extra £5 for cars meeting you at the airport and ferrying you into London).

Approximate taxi fares from
the airport to London W1 are:
Heathrow £40; Gatwick £70;
Stansted £94; City Airport £25.

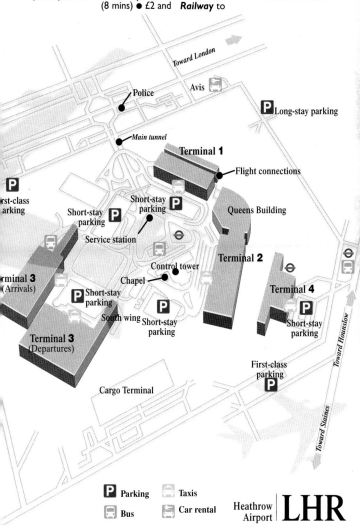

N↑

Stansted
40 miles
7 miles
LONDON · City Airport
Heathrow
15 miles
28 miles
Gatwick

Car rental
Avis
☎ (01279) 663 030
Hertz
☎ (01279) 680 154
Hotel
Hilton National
Round Copice
Road, Stansted,
Essex CM24 8SE
☎ (01279) 680800
➠ (01279) 680890

City
Airport

Information
☎ 0171-474 5555
Bus and train to
City Airport:
limited weekend
service.
Bus
Airport Shuttle
to Canary Wharf
(8 mins) ● £2 and

Liverpool Street
Station (25 mins)
● £4
Train
Bus to Canary
Wharf then
*Docklands
Railway* to

Bank (12 mins)
● £1.40
Car rental
Avis
☎ 0181-848 8733
Hertz
☎ 0181-679 1799

Toward London

● Police
● **P** Long-stay parking
● *Main tunnel*

Terminal 1
Flight connections

P First-class parking
Short-stay parking
Short-stay parking
Service station
Control tower
Queens Building

Chapel
Terminal 2

Terminal 3
(Arrivals)
P Short-stay parking
South wing Short-stay parking

Terminal 3
(Departures)

Terminal 4
P Short-stay parking

First-class parking
P

Cargo Terminal

Toward Hounslow
Toward Staines

P Parking   Taxis
Bus   Car rental

Heathrow
Airport **LHR**

9

The journey from Paris to London by *Eurostar* (1) takes 3 hours (2); 35 minutes to cross the Channel on *Le Shuttle* (3); around 3 hours by *ferry* from France to England (4); and 7 hours by *Orient Express* (5) or *coach*.

Getting there

eurostar

Ashford International

From the US

American Airlines
☎ UK
0345-789789
☎ US
800-433-7300
British Airways
☎ UK
0345 222111
☎ US
800-247-9297
Delta
☎ UK
0800-414767
☎ US
800-241-4141
Virgin Atlantic
☎ UK
(01293) 747747
☎ US
800-862-8621
British Airways and American Airlines offer direct flights from New York, Chicago and Los Angeles, Virgin and Delta offer direct flights from New York and Los Angeles. Flying times are approximately 7 hours from New York to London, 9 hours from Chicago and 10 to 12 hours from Los Angeles. Many airlines offer cheap last minute deals for flights from North America. (See pages 8–9 for information on traveling into central London from the airports.)

From Europe

London is easily accessible from almost every major European city. Most major airlines offer flights into at least one of London's international airports and there are train and shuttle services that will take you to London. The introduction of Eurostar and Le Shuttle (with its direct links with Paris, Brussels and Amsterdam), provides a fast and reasonably priced alternative to flying.

Eurostar

The journey by Eurostar from Gare du Nord in Paris to Waterloo Station in London via the Channel Tunnel takes just 3 hours. The journey to Brussels from Waterloo takes 3¼ hours. Some trains stop to pick up passengers at Calais Frethun, Lille Europe or Ashford International. During the week there are hourly departures from both Paris and London. The first Eurostar train reaches London before 9am; and Paris before 9am. The last train departs from Paris around 9pm and from London around 8pm. Parking lots are open from 5am to 1am at both stations. Waterloo is right in the

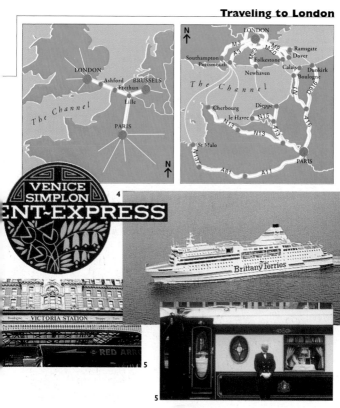

center of London (5 mins on foot from Big Ben), and is on the subway (Northern and Bakerloo lines).

Information / reservations
☎ 0990-300003
☎ 0345-303030

Le Shuttle

Le Shuttle service allows you to cross via the Channel Tunnel with a car; the journey takes 35 minutes. There are between three and four crossings per hour. Driving from Folkestone into London takes about 90 mins.

Information / reservations
Tickets are available from

tour operators, or can be bought at the terminal or reserved by telephone.
Shuttle Info
☎ 0990-353535

The Orient Express

Runs from March to November on Thursdays and some Sundays. It departs from Gare de l'Est in Paris at 9.45am, arriving at London Victoria at 4.55pm. There is also a red-carpet service on the Pullman Orient Express – a veritable luxury and extremely expensive.

Information / reservations
☎ 0171-805 5060

By boat

There are a number of ferry, hydrofoil and hovercraft services from Europe to the UK. Depending on where you are traveling from and whether you are taking a night crossing, journey times will range from 35 minutes to 24 hours. All UK ports are linked to central London by rail.

Information / reservations
Brittany Ferries
☎ 0803-828828
Hoverspeed
☎ 0990-240241
P & O Ferries
☎ 0990-980980
Stena Line
☎ 0990-707070

By coach

Eurolines offers coach trips between London and many major European cities. Journeys include a ferry crossing via Dover, Ramsgate, Portsmouth or Plymouth. But beware, despite the fact that coaches are now much improved and often provide a range of services, this can be a tedious and even expensive way to travel.

Information / reservations
☎ 0171-730 8235
For information on Hoverspeed, coach, hovercraft or hydrofoil call (01304) 240241.

Basic facts

London has the largest subway network in Europe. On the street, two vehicles are famous worldwide as symbols of London – the double-decker Routemaster bus and the black cab. Black-cab drivers train for three years and pass a testing exam on their knowledge of London's streets, so you

Getting around

The tube

The London subway, or 'tube', first opened in 1863 and is the oldest subway system in the world. Although increasingly prone to disruption and delays, the tube is still the fastest way to get around London.

Train times

The tube runs from around 5.30am to midnight (11.30pm on Sun.). Rush hour is around 8–9am and 5–6.30pm. Each station has a timetable for the different lines running from that station. Some stations are closed at weekends or during off-peak times. Information: ☎ 0171-222 1234

Tube lines

Each of London's tube lines is identified by a name and a color on the map. ➡ 170. At some stations, a number of lines operate from one platform. Always check the noticeboard for the train's destination.

Tickets

A one-zone ticket costs £1.20. Tickets and travelcards are available from underground ticket offices and some newsagents. There is an on-the-spot fine of £10 for those caught traveling without a ticket or with an incorrect ticket. Smoking is banned on the tube system: a fine of £1000 may be imposed for anyone caught smoking.

Travelcards

Daily, weekly and monthly travelcards are available for travel on tubes, trains and buses (1, 2, 4 or 6 zones). Travelcards are sold in subway stations and in newsagents (you will need a passport photo for weekly or monthly cards).

Bus

Traveling by bus is less expensive than the tube and offers better views of London. Bus rides often take longer than the tube and you may have to wait a while for a bus to arrive.

Taking the bus

Beware: some buses do not run the whole length of the route. Check the destination on the front of the bus before you get on. Ring the bell for the bus to pull up at your required stop. Bus maps are available from underground stations ➡ 170.

Bus times

Buses run from 5am to 11.30pm.

Night buses

Night buses run throughout the night from 11.30pm onward. All night buses

KENSINGTON
GORE **SW7**

CITY OF WESTMINSTER

can rely on them to get you there by the best route.

have the letter 'N' in front of the route number. Night bus routes cover the whole of the London area and services run until 6am. One-day travelcards are not valid on night buses.

Bus stops

Main ('fare stage') bus stops have a white sign. Buses will stop here automatically. Request stops have red signs. Buses will only pull in here if you signal the driver to stop.

Tickets

Buy a travelcard or pay for each ride individually (the cost varies according to the number of zones crossed). On

newer buses buy your ticket from the driver as you get on board. On older-style buses a bus conductor will sell you a ticket.

Taxis

The celebrated London cab provides a reliable, fast and comfortable service. Minicabs are less expensive than black cabs, but do not generally offer the same comfort or reliability.

Black cabs

There are taxi cab ranks at many of London's stations and black cabs can also be hailed in the street. Cabs are available when their 'For Hire' or

'Taxi' sign is lit up. Tell the driver your destination before getting in to the vehicle. The cost of the journey will be shown on the meter. A 10% tip on top of this is usual.

Dial-a-Cab
☎ 0171-253 5000

Minicabs

Minicabs are run by independent companies. To rent a minicab, you will need to go into the office in person, or reserve by telephone. Many minicab companies offer a 24-hour service. Always request a quote beforehand and ask what kind of car to expect.

Atlas Cars
☎ 0171-602 1234

By car

Driving and parking in London are not recommended.

Car rental

There are rental companies at airports and throughout London.

Parking

Parking in London is both difficult and expensive. Double yellow lines at the side of the road mean 'no parking'.

Regulations

Drive on the left and always fasten your seatbelt. Speed limit is 30mph in the city, 60mph on major roads and 70mph on freeways.

Gas

Available from gas stations and sold by the liter.

Basic facts

You can find most international publications on sale in the heart of Soho; St Martin's Lane post office is open until 8pm even on Saturday; the London Tourist Board offers a reservations service and has information on most events happening in the capital; the British Travel

Getting by

Money

You can take out cash or pay for goods on most international credit cards. The currency is the pound sterling (£), which is divided into 100 pence (p).

Exchange rates

£1 = US$1.6 (at time of going to press)
You can change cash or traveler's checks at all major banks and bureaux de changes on presentation of your passport or other accepted means of identification.
⊙ *Mon.–Fri. 9.30am–3.30pm, some branches are also open Sat. 10am–12.30pm.* Some hotels, stores and tour operators offer an exchange service and airport bureaux

de change are open 24 hours.

Tipping

A tip of 10 to 15% is the usual amount given to taxi drivers and in restaurants. Tipping is not usual in pubs.

Media

Newspapers

Many national daily and weekly newspapers are available, ranging from tabloids, such as *The Sun*, to broadsheets, for example, *The Times*. London's dedicated newspaper is *The Evening Standard*.

International press

You will find most international newspapers on sale in Soho in newsagents along Old Compton Street: *Capital Newsagent* and *The World's Daily Newspaper*.

Radio

BBC Radio 1 98.8mHz (FM); BBC Radio 2 89.1mHz (FM); BBC Radio 3 91.3mHz (FM); BBC Radio 4 93.5mHz (FM); BBC Radio 5 Live 330m/909kHz (MW); Classic FM 100.9mHz (FM).

Television

There are five terrestrial channels: *BBC1*, *BBC2*, *ITV*, *Channel 4* and *Channel 5*.

Telephone

Dialing codes

London numbers are preceded by either 0171 or 0181. You will need to dial the code when telephoning from one zone to another, but not if you are calling within the same zone.

To call the US from Britain

Dial 00 + 1 + the local code and number you require.

Operator services

Operator: ☎ 100
International operator: ☎ 155
Directory enquiries: ☎ 192
International information: ☎ 153

Public telephones

Public telephones take 10p, 20p, 50p and £1 coins or telephone cards, available from post offices, newsagents and stores displaying the "Phonecard" sign. Some telephones also take credit cards.

International telephone cards

Fun Card (Sprint) and *Calling Card* (AT&T) will allow

Centre has information covering the whole of the UK; London also has a lost property office.

you to make calls on an account.
SPRINT
🆅 *0800-195005*
AT&T
🆅 *0800-485111*

Internet

Many of London's major hotels offer internet facilities and there are internet cafés throughout the city, such as:

Cyberia
39 Whitfield Street, W1
☎ *0171-209 0982*
➡ *0171-209 0984*
@ *cyberia@ easynet.co.uk*
🕐 *Mon.–Fri. 11am–10pm; Sat.–Sun. 10am–9pm*

Mail

Many hotels offer a postal service to guests.

Post offices

🕐 *Mon.–Fri. 9am–5.30pm, Sat. 9am–1pm*
The post office on St Martin's Lane (near Trafalgar Square) is open until 8pm, even on Saturday.
24–28 William IV Street, WC2
☎ *0171-930 9580*

Stamps

There are two postal rates: first-class stamps (26p) and second-class stamps (20p). A postcard stamp to North America costs 37p.

Alcohol

In the UK it is illegal to sell alcohol to anyone under 18 years of age. Alcohol is available from stores, supermarkets and off-licences.

24-hour opening

7 Eleven are open daily and sell everything from newspapers and tobacco to groceries. Many stores in London open on Sundays.

Tourist offices

London Tourist Board
Victoria Station Forecourt, SW1
☎ *0839-123456*
🕐 *daily. 8am–7pm*
Information on everything that is happening in London.

British Travel Centre
4-12 Regent Street, SW1
☎ *0181-846 9000*
🕐 *Mon.–Fri. 9am–6.30pm; Sat.–Sun. 10am–4pm*
Information on the whole of the UK.

Lost property

Lost Property, 200 Baker Street, NW1
☎ *0171-486 2496*
🕐 *Mon.–Fri. 9.30am–2pm*
For items lost on London transport.

Emergency services

Police, fire service, ambulance

☎ *999 or 112*
24-hour service. Calls are free.

Hospitals

London has a number of National Health Service (NHS) and private hospitals. European Union and some Commonwealth country citizens will be treated free; American and Canadian travelers should take out medical insurance.

Dental emergencies

☎ *0171-837 3646*

Pharmacies

Bliss Chemist
5 Marble Arch, W1
☎ *0171-723 6116*
🕐 *daily 9am–midnight*

Hotel restaurants

London's leading hotels were once the only places to enjoy high-quality food. These hotel restaurants ➡ 42 are still numbered among the best in the city.

Where to stay

Beware!

Staying in a London hotel can be very expensive. It is difficult to find reasonable accommodation for less than £70, and you are advised to book rather than trying to find something when you arrive.

Prices The following information is given for each hotel: number of rooms and price range; number of suites and top price; cost of the least expensive breakfast (continental breakfast). Prices are excluding value added tax (17.5%). Room prices are for double rooms. Single rooms are usually slightly less expensive depending on the season and length of stay. Be warned: hotels in London tend to be expensive.

54
Hotels

THE INSIDER'S FAVORITES

Bed & breakfast

Staying in a B&B or guest house is an economic way to stay in London. Tourist offices will provide you with a list of guest houses throughout the London area ➡ 14. Prices vary greatly but will generally be less than hotel prices. Reserve well in advance, depending on how close to the center of town you wish to stay.

Youth hostels

London has several youth hostels, which are for the young and for members of the Youth Hostel Association. Reserve in advance. For information contact:
YHA ☎ 0171-248 6547
🕐 Mon.–Fri. 9am–5.30pm

Covent Garden is the heart of theaterland and a lively shopping area. Soho is London's major restaurant area. ■ Where to eat ➡ 44 ➡ 46 ➡ 48 ➡ 50 ■ After dark ➡ 82 ➡ 86 ➡ 90 ➡ 92 ➡ 94 ■ What to see ➡ 102 ■ Where to shop ➡ 140 ➡ 142 ➡ 144 ➡ 160

Where to stay

Covent Garden Hotel (1)
10 Monmouth Street, WC2 ☎ 0171-806 1000 ➡ 0171-806 1100

⊖ Covent Garden, Leicester Square *47 rooms* ●●● ▢ *3 suites £305* 🏵 *£9.50* ⓪ 🖭⊖ 📠 📇 Ⓨ 🎏 @ *firmdale@dircon.co.uk*

This hotel was recently opened by Tim and Kit Kemp and has rapidly become an extremely popular hotel for those wishing to stay in the Covent Garden area. From the entrance hall with a brasserie to one side to the stone staircase that leads up to a large drawing room and library, the emphasis is on strong colors, sumptuous hand-embroidered Eastern fabrics, wood and stone – all creating a stunning interior to this lofty converted 1865 building. Those who enjoy theatrical settings should ask for the two-story, high-ceilinged Loft Suite with gallery bedroom and dressing room, fireplace, separate book-lined study and two bathrooms.

Hazlitt's (2)
6 Frith Street, W1 ☎ 0171-434 1771 ➡ 0171-439 1524

⊖ Leicester Square *22 rooms* ●●● *1 suite £217* ▢ *Closed Dec. 25–26* 🏵 *£7.30* ▢ 🖭 🗴

The Soho streets are filled with 20th-century life, but behind Hazlitt's Georgian façade, the 18th-century London life lingers on. An authentic decor of dark wood-paneled walls, creaking staircases, rooms all of differing sizes furnished with leather sofas, old prints and four-poster or half-tester beds plus a quiet lounge with fireplace, attracts the fashionable media crowd who appreciate its theatricality – as well as the thoroughly modern essentials such as good bathrooms and comfortable beds.

The Savoy (3)
Strand, WC2 ☎ 0171-836 4343 ➡ 0171-872 8901

⊖ Embankment, Charing Cross 🛐 *154 rooms* ●●●●● ▢ *48 suites £360* 🏵 *£13.25* ⓪ ▢ 🖭 📠 📇 Ⅲ 🎏 *River Restaurant, Savoy Grill, Upstairs at the Savoy* Ⓨ *American Bar* 🎏 *Thames Foyer* 🗴 🗴 ✚ 🗴 🗴 🎏 🗴 @ *www.savoy*

The Savoy (next door to the Savoy Theatre) was first opened in 1889 by Richard D'Oyly Carte who wanted somewhere for his actors and guests to stay. It is now fully renovated and brought up to date. But this grand London hotel also maintains the grace of the past, manifested in the splendid marble entrance hall, the beautiful bedrooms with their art deco touches and the excellent Savoy service. The views from the riverside rooms, which inspired the French Impressionist painter Monet to capture the seasons on the Thames on canvas, remain as impressive as ever. Tradition also remains in The American Bar (still one of London's best-known meeting places), in the Thames Foyer (serving afternoon tea), in the River Restaurant and the Grill (recommended for dinner), and, finally, in the legendary Savoy wine cellars.

Not forgetting
■ **The Meridien Waldorf** (4) Aldwych, WC2 ☎ 0171-836 2400 ➡ 0171-836 7244 ●●●●●

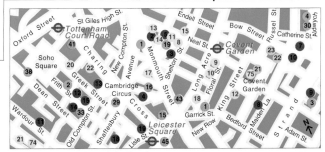

The Savoy boasts a magnificent main entrance, tucked away just south of the Strand. Doormen and chauffeurs stand at the ready.

19

Home to gentlemen's clubs, bespoke boot- and hat-makers, wine merchants and restaurants, the air here is of old, aristocratic London. ■ Where to eat ➡ 52 ➡ 54 ■ After dark ➡ 86 ➡ 90 ■ What to see ➡ 104 ➡ 118 ■ Where to shop ➡ 146 ➡ 148 ➡ 150

➡ Where to stay

22 Jermyn Street (5)
22 Jermyn Street, SW1 ☎ 0171-734 2353 ➡ 0171-734 0750

🔵 Piccadilly Circus 🅿 **5 rooms ●●●●** 13 suites £270 🔲 £10.50 ▨ ⓪ ☎ ▥ ⟲ ⚎ ➕ ✖ @ www.22jermyn.com

Just south of Piccadilly, behind a discreet doorway in quiet Jermyn Street, full of bespoke tailors and shirt-makers, lies this top-quality, small hotel. Its old-style club-like, sophisticated welcome can be attributed to the ubiquitous presence of Henry Togna whose family have owned the hotel since 1915, and to a staff who could not be more helpful. The added luxury of period furniture, sumptuous fabrics, antiques and fireplaces in rooms and suites create the atmosphere of an elegant house rather than a hotel, while the extensive range of business services satisfies the most demanding tycoon.

The Stafford (6)
16–18 St James's Place, SW1 ☎ 0171-493 0111 ➡ 0171-493 7121

🔵 Green Park 🅿 **67 rooms ●●●●** 13 suites £450 🔲 £13.50 ▨ ⓪ ▤ ☎ ▥ ⬚ ⌇ The Stafford Restaurant, The American Bar 🍸 ⚎ ✖ @ info@ thestaffordhotel.co.uk

A gem of a hotel in its own courtyard off busy St James's Street and a haven of civilized calm. Following the hotel's refurbishment, The Stafford's many devotees are returning to experience once more the feeling of entering a private house, rather than a hotel. Of particular note are the delightful, antique-filled small entrance hall and drawing room, luxurious, English-style bedrooms and the 370-year old wine cellars which are available for private parties. The American Bar has been one of London's most popular venues for decades. The rooms in the carriage house offer greater privacy, tucked in a cobbled yard that evokes the days of London's coaching inns.

Dukes Hotel (7)
35 St James's Place, SW1 ☎ 0171-491 4840 ➡ 0171-493 1264

🔵 Green Park 🅿 **52 rooms ●●●●** 12 suites £264 🔲 £9.50 ▨ ⓪ ☎ ▥ ⟲ ⌇ 🍸 ⚎ ✖ ➕ ⛃ @ 106161.101@compuserve.com

Hidden away in a small flower-filled courtyard right in the heart of St James's, the Edwardian, red-brick Dukes Hotel resembles a grand old private town house. All is in keeping: a grandfather clock chimes out the hours in the hallway; antique furniture, along with Spode or Bow china, fills the attractive, individually decorated bedrooms and a butler is available for guests. One further compelling reason to stay at Dukes is the club-like bar – renowned for its collection of Cognacs and the knowledgeable barman, Gilberto.

■ **The Cavendish (8)** 81 Jermyn Street, SW1 ☎ 0171-930 2111 ➡ 0171-839 2125 ●●●

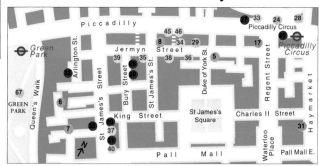

London's quality hotels specialize in providing guests with an attentive, personal service. The rooms are often individual in character and each room may have a name as well as a number, such as the Dukes Hotel, where seven of the rooms are named after grand dukes.

22 JERMYN STREET

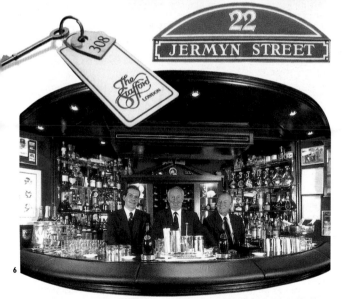

DUKES
HOTEL

21

Mayfair has always been frequented by the wealthy and the area around Bond Street, Savile Row and Cork Street still offers good shopping for art, menswear and fashion names, as well as a number of top hotels.

■ Where to eat ➡ 58 ■ After dark ➡ 84 ■ What to see ➡ 118

Where to stay

Claridge's (9)
Brook Street, W1 ☎ 0171-629 8860 ➡ 0171-499 2210

🔵 *Bond Street* 🅿 *141 rooms* ●●●●● *56 suites £480* 📶 *£13.50* ▢ ⓪ ▣
📞 Ⅲ▷ 🛗 Ⅲ 🍴 *The Restaurant, The Causerie, The Orangery* 🍸 *The Foyer* 🍵
The Reading Room 🏋 ✖ ✚ 🎿 ◉ ✳

Guests entering the elegant hallway with its black-and-white marbled floor and sweeping staircase follow in the footsteps of the heads of state, royal families, the famous and the discerning that Claridge's has been welcoming for more than a century. Newly created magnificent penthouses and the health center have been designed in keeping with the art deco style of the original Edwardian hotel. Tradition lives on in the famous, pink-washed art deco restaurant designed in 1926 by Basil Ionides, in the priceless antiques and original molding in the bedrooms, in the Reading Room where liveried footmen serve afternoon tea, in the Foyer where cocktails are served, in the Causerie where guests enjoy informal lunches and dinners, and in the impeccable Claridge's service.

47 Park Street (10)
47 Park Street, W1 ☎ 0171-491 7282 ➡ 0171-491 7281

🔵 *Marble Arch* 🅿 *52 suites* ●●●●● 📶 *£13.50* ▢ ⓪ ▣ 📞 Ⅲ▷ 🛗 Ⅲ
🍴 *Le Gavroche* ➡ 58 🏋 ✖ ✚

Originally built as a town house in 1926 by the first Baron Milford, 47 Park Street is now an expensive, chic, French-owned hotel which delights in providing the highest standards to those who stay there. There are no individual rooms, only 52 antique-filled suites, each with their own fully equipped kitchens for private entertainment, though the presence of one of London's top restaurants, Le Gavroche, on its premises and 24-hour room service from those kitchens might discourage all but the most enthusiastic.

The Connaught (11)
16 Carlos Place, W1 ☎ 0171-499 7070 ➡ 0171-495 3262

🔵 *Bond Street, Green Park* *66 rooms* ●●●●● *24 suites £670* 📶 *£15*
▢ ⓪ 📞 Ⅲ▷ 🍴 *The Grill Room, The Connaught Restaurant* ➡ 60 🍸 🏋 ✖ ✚
@ *info@thconnaught.co.uk*

An air of discreet, dignified elegance fills The Connaught, so well established among the world's sophisticated travelers that it has no need to advertise its privacy and tranquility. The Edwardian hotel is formal and old-fashioned in atmosphere, retaining a grand baronial-style wooden staircase, wooden paneling, plaster ceilings, large marble fireplaces, antiques in each of the bedrooms and a rich, aristocratic decor throughout. The English manor-house style lives on at The Connaught, even down to the long-serving staff who offer the gracious hospitality and impeccable service reminiscent of a seemingly bygone age.

■ Where
to shop
➡ 152

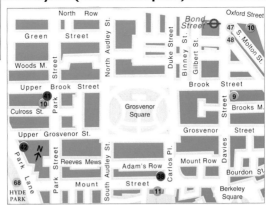

Open to non-residents, good
hotels are an ideal choice for a
delicious lunch, dinner, afternoon
tea or simply an aperitif.

In the area

Looking out over Hyde Park, Park Lane forms the western border to Mayfair with many of London's top hotels located around Hyde Park Corner. ■ Where to eat ➡ 56 ➡ 58 ■ After dark ➡ 92 ■ What to see ➡ 104 ➡ 118 ■ Where to shop ➡ 150 ➡ 152

➡ Where to stay

Brown's (12)
30 Albemarle Street, W1 ☎ 0171-493 6020 ➡ 0171-493 9381

🔵 Green Park 🅿 *118 rooms* ●●●●● *7 suites £460* 🔲 *£12* ▫ 🔘 ▪ ☎ 🔲 Ⅰ▶
🔳 🔳 *Brown's Restaurant* 🔳 *St George's* 🔲 *The Lounge* 🔳 ✖ ✚

Brown's, which runs between Dover and Albemarle streets, remains as chintzy, comfortable, quiet and traditional as it was in Queen Victoria's day. The bedrooms and suites follow this particularly English style with floral-patterned furnishings and the occasional four-poster bed; downstairs there is wooden paneling throughout, ornate period plastered ceilings and sumptuous flower arrangements. At any time, the club-like St George's Bar is full while the delightful drawing room, complete with crackling fires, large sofas and wing chairs plays host to transatlantic families and parties of ladies settling down to traditional afternoon tea.

The Dorchester (13)
53 Park Lane, W1 ☎ 0171-629 8888 ➡ 0171-409 0114

🔵 Hyde Park Corner 🅿 *192 rooms* ●●●●● *52 suites £470* 🔲 *£15.50* ▫ 🔘
▪ ☎ Ⅰ▶ 🔳 ⅠⅠⅠ 🔳 *The Grill Room, The Oriental, The Promenade* 🔲 🔳 ✖ ✚
🔳 🔳 🔲

A hotel to see and also one to be seen in, The Dorchester glitters and gleams, from the twinkling lights in the tree outside to the magnificent gilded entrance way and marble-pillared promenade. The style throughout this impeccably restored hotel is a wonderful mix of English country-house antiques and Chinoiserie. Style and panache reach their height in the Oliver Messel suite, originally completed in 1952 and named after the brilliant theater designer. Overlooking Hyde Park, the hotel attracts some of the world's most famous and glamorous characters.

Four Seasons Hotel (14)
Hamilton Place, Park Lane W1
☎ 0171-499 0888 ➡ 0171-493 6629

🔵 Hyde Park Corner, Green Park 🅿 *227 rooms* ●●●●● *26 suites £587* 🔲
£13.75 ▫ 🔘 ▪ ☎ Ⅰ▶ 🔳 🔳 *The Four Seasons, The Lanes Restaurant*
🔲 *The Lounge* 🔳 *£17.50* 🔳 ✖ ✚ 🔳 🔳 🔳

The hotel may be recent, but the beautiful interior is decorated in traditional style. Lofty and airy, the public rooms are fitted out in rich woods and have marble floors. Grace and space characterize the Four Seasons Hotel chain, a top international group offering amenities that are hard to match.

Not forgetting

■ **The Metropolitan (15)** 19 Old Park Lane, W1 ☎ 0171-447 1000 ➡ 0171-447 1100 @ sales@metropolitan.co.uk ●●●●
■ **The Park Lane Hotel (16)** Piccadilly, W1 ☎ 0171-499 6321 ➡ 0171-499 1965 ●●●●

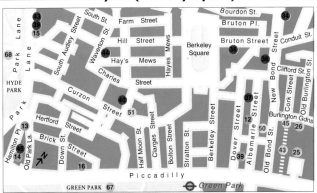

Bourdon St.
South St.   Bruton Pl.
34
39 Farm   Street   Bruton Street
15   Conduit St.
Hill   Street   Berkeley 35
68   Square   36
Hay's Mews   New Bond Street
Charles   Clifford St.
Street   Cork Street
Curzon   Street   37   Old Burlington St.
HYDE   12   Burlington Gdns
PARK   40 51   50   45   26
Hertford Street   43   25
13
Brick St. Down St.   39 Albemarle St.
45 14 16   Old Bond St.
Piccadilly
GREEN PARK 67   ⊖ Green Park

Brown's has two entrances: one on Stratton
Street, the other on Albemarle Street. The first
was said to be the courtesans' entrance and the
other the entrance for the hotel guests.

12

13

13

13

13

14

In the area

Centered around Victoria station and stretching from Buckingham Palace in the north, over the river into Pimlico, Victoria is a residential area full of small hotels. It is close to parks in the north and also to the Thames, with Westminster Bridge to the east and Chelsea Bridge to the south.

Where to stay

The Goring (17)
15 Beeston Place, SW1 ☎ 0171-396 9000 ➡ 0171-834 4393

⊖ Victoria 🅿 **76 rooms** ●●● *3 suites £305* 🈂 *£10.75* 🔲 🕐 🔳 🈺 🍴 *The Dining Room* 🈂 ❎ ❌ ✚ ❎ ♒

This charming hotel could pass for an annex to Buckingham Palace. Family-owned since it was built by the Gorings in 1910, it is used by those invited to garden parties at the palace. Beyond the delightful hallway stretches a drawing room with a fireplace which crackles invitingly in winter as afternoon tea is served. Antiques and classical reproductions hang in the bedrooms and some rooms even have balconies looking out over the private garden. Very British, slightly formal but thoroughly welcoming.

Tophams Belgravia (18)
28 Ebury Street, SW1 ☎ 0171-730 8147 ➡ 0171-823 5966

⊖ Victoria **40 rooms** ●● 🈂 *free for guests* 🔲 *Closed Dec. 24–30* 🔳 🈺 ⏸ 🍴 *Tophams* 🈂 *Ebury Club* ✚ @ *10610.1706@compuserve.com*

Converted into a hotel 60 years ago, this establishment has always been run by the Tophams family. The haphazard plan to its corridors and stairs (it was originally five houses) adds to its charm. It has an old-fashioned style with candlewick bedspreads and pieces of china decorating the rooms. Guests can use the Ebury Club bar.

Elizabeth Hotel (19)
37 Eccleston Square, SW1 ☎ 0171-828 6812 ➡ 0171-828 6814

⊖ Victoria **38 rooms** ● 🈂 *£3, free for guests* 🈺 🔳 ✴ ♒

Set back from the road behind a pretty façade in a historic square, this simple, traditionally decorated hotel with the feel of a family guest house is welcoming and friendly with well-kept bedrooms. A predominantly light color scheme of beiges and creams adds space even in the smaller rooms. Breakfast is served downstairs in a pleasant area; on the first floor one decent sized drawing room has comfortable sofas and long windows opening onto the square.

The Windermere (20)
142–144 Warwick Way, SW1 ☎ 0171-834 5163 ➡ 0171-630 8831

⊖ Victoria **23 rooms** ● 🈂 *free for guests* 🔲 🔳 🈺 🍴 🈂 @ *100773.1171@compuserve.com*

A pretty, early Victorian building, the light, airy rooms (particularly those with windows on two sides) are well decorated with facilities many small hotels lack – satellite television, tea- and coffee-making facilities and hairdryers. The owners are invariably there to welcome or help.

Not forgetting
■ **Melbourne House (21)** 79 Belgrave Road, SW1 ☎ 0171-828 3516 ➡ 0171-828 7120 ●

What to see ➡ 110 ➡ 118

17

17

19

17

19

WINDERMERE

20

A delightful mix of embassies, stores, some small, others top designer names in Sloane Street, combined with residential areas around garden squares, and very smart hotels. ■ Where to eat ➡ 60 ■ After dark ➡ 92 ■ What to see ➡ 118 ■ Where to shop ➡ 138 ➡ 154

Where to stay

The Lanesborough (22)
Hyde Park Corner, SWI ☎ 0171-259 5599 ➡ 0171-259 5606

🌐 Hyde Park Corner 🅿 **49 rooms** ●●●●● 46 suites £470 🈯 £13 ▣ ⓞ ▣
🔲 ▥ 🔛 ▦ The Conservatory 🌀 🍴 🍽 ✚ 🍸 🍹

On arrival, guests are presented with their own personalized stationery and business cards – a service which sums up The Lanesborough. Among the world's most luxurious hotels, it caters to every need with each guest assigned a traditional butler who unpacks, irons and even runs baths. A neoclassical 1828 building on Hyde Park Corner, whose atmosphere is more that of a palace than a hotel; marbled corridors open on to beautiful public rooms full of sumptuous flower arrangements. First-floor rooms have fireplaces. Fabulously decorated bedrooms are equipped with state-of-the-art facilities, comfort and ease being paramount.

The Berkeley (23)
Wilton Place, SWI ☎ 0171-235 6000 ➡ 0171-235 4330

🌐 Hyde Park Corner 🅿 **157 rooms** ●●●●● 27 suites £580 🈯 £12.50 ▣ ⓞ
▣ 🔲 ▥ 🔛 ▥ ▦ The Berkeley, Vong 🌀 🍴 🍽 ✚ 🍸 🌊 🍹

A discreet hotel whose famous clientele come here to remain anonymous and enjoy the quiet elegance of the place. The feeling of spaciousness begins in the hallway with its open fireplace and magnificent flower arrangements and continues through the drawing rooms and the antique-filled bedrooms. With the only rooftop pool in London, opening up to the sky, exceptional views over Hyde Park, and trendsetting Thai restaurant, Vong ➡ 60, The Berkeley attracts an interesting cross-section of guests.

The Halkin (24)
5 Halkin Street, SWI ☎ 0171-333 1000 ➡ 0171-333 1100

🌐 Hyde Park Corner 🅿 **30 rooms** ●●●●● 11 suites £440 🈯 £9.50
▣ ⓞ ▣ 🔲 ▥ 🔛 ▦ The Halkin 🌀 🍴 🍽 ✚ 🍹 @ sales@halkin.co.uk

The Halkin is one of the new wave of hotels to open recently in London. In contrast to the traditional cozy English style of hotel, the Halkin possesses an atmosphere of chic minimalism and advanced technology. Exciting and innovative, it is decorated throughout in a highly sophisticated Italian design using granite, marble, and beautiful cherrywood, mahogany or rosewood. Even the entrance has automatically opening glass doors; such high-tech standards continue in the modern-style bedrooms. Stylish, cosmopolitan with one of the best restaurants (known simply as The Halkin ➡ 60) in London – be sure to pack something classy to wear.

Not forgetting
■ **The Mandarin Oriental Hyde Park (25)** 66 Knightsbridge, SWI
☎ 0171-235 2000 ➡ 0171-235 4552 ●●●●●

29

In the area

Knightsbridge was originally totally residential. The streets and small squares around Harrods are full of large, grand houses some of which have since been converted into some magnificent, upmarket, town-house hotels. Nowadays people come here mainly to shop. ■ Where to eat

➤ Where to stay

Knightsbridge Green (26)
159 Knightsbridge, SW1 ☎ 0171-584 6274 ➠ 0171-225 1635

🔵 *Knightsbridge* 🅿 *15 rooms* ●● *12 suites £145* 💷 *£6* ▭ *Closed Dec. 24–26* ▣ ☎ ▥ ▢ @ *theKGHotel@aol.com*

Staff at this Knightsbridge hotel are very welcoming and helpful. An elevator will take you up to the delightfully decorated, uncluttered and large bedrooms.

The Capital (27)
22 Basil Street, SW3 ☎ 0171-589 5171 ➠ 0171-225 0011

🔵 *Knightsbridge* 🅿 *48 rooms* ●●●●● *8 suites £365* 💷 *£12.50* ▭ ◉ ▣ ☎ ▥ ⬛ ▥ ⫿ *The Capital Restaurant* ▼ ✖ ✖ ✚

Intimate and luxurious, The Capital bears the hallmarks of a privately owned hotel: guest umbrellas, fruit bowls in the English-style bedrooms, and wines from the owners' own French vineyard. Bathrooms are first-rate, the hotel's atmosphere is warm and the service attentive.

The Beaufort (28)
33 Beaufort Gardens, SW3 ☎ 0171-584 5252 ➠ 0171-589 2834

🔵 *Knightsbridge* *28 rooms* ●●●● *7 suites £285* 💷 *£7.50* ▭ ◉ *7am–9pm* ▣ ☎ ▥ ▥ ▼ ✖ ✖ ✚ ⬇

In a quiet street, this small country-house hotel claims that some of the world's largest business deals were created there. Extras include cream teas and 24-hour champagne – maybe to celebrate the latest deal.

The Cliveden Town House (29)
26 Cadogan Gardens, SW3 ☎ 0171-730 6466 ➠ 0171-730 0236

🔵 *Sloane Square* *35 rooms* ●●●● *3 suites £365* 💷 *£12.50* ▭ ◉ ☎ ▥ ⬛ ▥ ✖ ✖ ⬇

The scent of apples, piled in two stone urns, gives this hotel something of the atmosphere of the pied-à-terre of a farmer. The spacious rooms are decorated with antique furniture.

The Sloane Hotel (30)
29 Draycott Place, SW3 ☎ 0171-581 5757 ➠ 0171-584 1348

🔵 *Sloane Square* *12 rooms* ●●● *3 suites £265* 💷 *£9* ▭ ◉ ▣ ☎ ▥ ✖ ✚ ⬇

Behind its classic Victorian façade this hotel is full of antiques – all of which, from the tapestries and paintings to the beds, are for sale. There are surprising extras – a rooftop lounge terrace with views over Chelsea.

Not forgetting

■ **The Cadogan (31)** 75 Sloane Street, SW1 ☎ 0171-235 7141 ➠ 0171-245 0994 ●●● ■ **Eleven Cadogan Gardens (32)** 11 Cadogan Gardens, SW3 ☎ 0171-730 3426 ➠ 0171-730 5217 ●●●

➡ 60 ➡ 68 ▬ Where to shop ➡ 138
➡ 154 ➡ 156

28

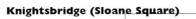

30

27

29

26

In the area

One of London's most sought-after residential areas, South Kensington comprises main streets lined with mansion blocks and tiny side streets full of interesting houses. The top town-house hotels, which are converted private houses, fit in beautifully, offering visitors the feeling of

Where to stay

The Gore Hotel (33)
189 Queen's Gate, SW7 ☎ 0171-584 6601 ➡ 0171-589 8127

🚇 Gloucester Road 🅿 **48 rooms** ●●● 6 suites £260 📺 £5.95 ⬛ 🖥 📷 📠
🍴 Bistro, Downstairs 🍷 ♻ ✗ ♨

Under the same ownership as Hazlitt's ➡ 18, the Gore is decorated in rich greens and reds and is full of potted plants, objets d'art and Victorian paintings. Those who prefer can reserve the Tudor Room, or the Venus Room for its gilded bed and neoclassical theme. Ornate and comfortable, the Gore has a splendid lounge, and two good restaurants.

Five Sumner Place (34)
5 Sumner Place, SW7 ☎ 0171-584 7586 ➡ 0171-823 9962

🚇 South Kensington 🅿 **13 rooms** ●● 📺 free to residents ⬛ 🖥 📷 📠 ✴ @
No.5@dial.piper.com

Built in the same style as the neighboring houses, this charming hotel, with its friendly staff and rear courtyard where breakfast is served, feels more like a private house than a hotel. The larger rooms look out onto the street, the smaller ones have a rooftop view.

Sydney House (35)
9–11 Sydney Street, SW3 ☎ 0171-376 7711 ➡ 0171-376 4233

🚇 South Kensington **21 rooms** ●●●● 📺 £8.50 ⬛ 🕐 🖥 📷 📠 🍷 ♻ ✗ ✴

Sydney House brings something new and distinctive to town-house hotel design. Each bedroom, individually designed by Swiss owner, designer and hotelier Jean-Luc Aeby, is different in style. Guests can choose from the Chinese Leopard Room (Biedermeier furniture, yellows and golds), the Wedgwood Blue Room (classical, blue and white) or the Paris Room (Toile de Jouy, reds and scarlets). Friendly service.

The CRANLEY

Blakes Hotel (36)
33 Roland Gardens, SW7 ☎ 0171-370 6701 ➡ 0171-373 0442

🚇 South Kensington, Gloucester Road **51 rooms** ●●●●● 📺 £13.75 ⬛ 🕐 🖥
📷 📠 📠 🍴 Blakes Restaurant 🍷 ✴

Fashion designer and hotelier Anouska Hempel has created a series of rooms ranging from the Oriental to the Venetian which are complete with *trompe l'oeil*, draped beds, silks and velvets, and gilded furniture. Guests can gather in the small foyer, with its natural wood and bamboo, eat predominantly oriental at Blakes Restaurant or in the intimate Chinese Room, an alcove filled with lacquerware and silks.

Not forgetting

■ **The Pelham (37)** 15 Cromwell Place, SW7 ☎ 0171-589 8288 ➡ 0171-584 8444 ●●● ■■ **Number Sixteen (38)** 16 Sumner Place, SW7 ☎ 0171-589 5232 ➡ 0171-584 8615 ●●● ■■ **The Cranley (39)** 10-12 Bina Gardens, SW5 ☎ 0171-373 0123 ➡ 0171-373 9497 ●●●

being part of London life.
- ■ Where to eat ➡ 62 ➡ 68
- ■ After dark ➡ 88 ■ What to see ➡ 114 ➡ 118

KENSINGTON GARDENS

HYDE PARK

"The Ring"

Kensington Road

De Vere Gdns

Palace Gate

Hyde Park Ga.

Queen's Gate

Kensington Gore

Prince Consort Rd

Queen's Gate Terr.

Elvaston Place

Queen's Gate Gardens

Gloucester Road

Q u e e n ' s   G a t e

E x h i b i t i o n   R o a d

C r o m w e l l   R o a d

Gloucester Road

Stanhope Gdns

Clareville St.

Bina Gdns

Drayton Gardens

Creswell Place

Old Brompton Road

Roland Gdns

Cranley Gardens

Onslow Gardens

Foulis Terr.

Sumner Pl.

F u l h a m   R o a d

South Parade

Cale St.

Sydney St.

Thurloe Place

Thurloe Square

South Kensington

Pelham St.

Onslow Square

Pond Place

69 58 68 60 59 21 33 56 57 55 37 39 38 34 35 36 71

34

39

33

36

35

35

To the southwest, the Kensington area, with its numerous small stores and hotels, merges into Earl's Court around the Exhibition Centre. The northern side borders London's major museum area and Hyde Park ➡ 118. The area is filled with small green squares and boasts three of

Where to stay

The Amber Hotel (40)
101 Lexham Gardens, W8 ☎ 0171-373 8666 ➡ 0171-835 1194

Ⓔ Earl's Court 🅿 **40 rooms** ● 🌱 free to residents ▯ ▯ ☎ 📺 ⭐ ⛷

Scandinavian-owned, impeccably kept and looking out at the back over a series of pretty private gardens, the Amber Hotel is a genuine find and extraordinarily good value for money. Breakfast, served in the downstairs dining room, is generous buffet style. Other plus points at this hotel include a warm welcome and the well-appointed bedrooms, all of them quiet, comfortable, well decorated and with stunning bathrooms. The Amber is situated in a quiet residential street, within easy walking distance of the stores and museums in Cromwell Road and South Kensington.

The Amsterdam (41)
7 Trebovir Road, SW5 ☎ 0171-370 5084 ➡ 0171-244 7608

Ⓔ Earl's Court 🅿 **20 rooms** ● 5 suites £75 🌱 free to residents ▯ ☎ ✖ ✗ ⭐

This busy hotel is located in a wide street, close to the lively Earl's Court area. The Amsterdam is decorated throughout in delicate pastel shades and has attractive pictures hanging on the walls. Some of the rooms have balconies overlooking gardens; others are generously sized and would comfortably sleep a family of four. Service is very helpful and friendly, breakfast is continental style and the hotel prices are extremely competitive.

The Rushmore (42)
11 Trebovir Road, SW5
☎ 0171-370 3839 / 0171-370 6505 ➡ 0171-370 0274

Ⓔ Earl's Court **22 rooms** ●● 30 apartments £280 per week 🌱 free to guests
▯ ▯ ☎ ✗

Like the Amsterdam Hotel, the Rushmore is very reasonably priced and stands in an impressive Kensington town house overlooking a busy residential street. The hotel is beautifully decorated and filled with nooks and crannies and unusual features such as Italian stencil pictures on the walls, candlesticks on tables, and attic rooms. The functional bathrooms are decorated in marble and copper and immaculately kept. Comfortable and well maintained, the Rushmore offers various facilities and services that you would not generally expect in a hotel of this category. For business guests, there is even a conference room for meetings, and secretarial services available on request. Buffet-style breakfast is served in the first-floor dining room where the Italian-style theme is continued with its decor of stone and granite floors and wrought-iron furniture. For guests planning longer stays the Rushmore also has several apartments available to rent in the area. It is best to reserve well in advance and to ask about the different types of accommodation available.

the least expensive hotels in London.
A quiet, calm, and fairly central area.

■ Where to eat ➡ 64

40

40

41

41

In the area

London's literary area in the days of the novelist Virginia Woolf and friends, Bloomsbury remains an intellectual center, dominated by the British Museum and the University of London, small museums and antiquarian bookstores. ■ Where to eat ➡ 44 ➡ 72 ■ What to see

Where to stay

The Generator (43)
MacNaughten House, Compton Place, WCI
☎ 0171-388 7666 ➡ 0171-388 7644

🔵 *Russell Square* **210 rooms** ● 📋 *free to residents* 🔲 📶

Unusual to say the least, The Generator is a great hostel for the young. Tucked into a small courtyard, it's an old police section house with a high-tech interior in the main public areas, which go under the names of The Fuel Stop, R & R, The Chiller and Talking Heads. Bedrooms are basic, with bunk beds, washbasins and mirrors provided; showers are shared. It's fun, funky and extraordinarily good value, with singles at £32.50 and four sharing at £17 per person. A great place, leaving its guests enough spare cash to enjoy London's music and club scene.

The Academy (44)
21 Gower Street, WCI ☎ 0171-631 4115 ➡ 0171-636 3442

🔵 *Goode Street, Russell Square* 🅿 **36 rooms** ●● *5 suites £160* 📋 *£6.95* 🔲
🔲 📺 🏧 🛗 🍴 *GHQ* 📶 ✖ ✳

This well-established Bloomsbury hotel has been growing in popularity, and in size, for many years. Three houses are joined together to form a delightful, well decorated, comfortable and, thanks to efficient facilities, very quiet hotel. Bedrooms are luxurious, many with half-tester beds and beautiful swags of material, and bathrooms are of an exceptional standard for a small hotel. There's a small library leading into a garden and a downstairs bar and restaurant, GHQ. The pictures are a feature here, adding to the hotel's very personal touch.

Blooms Hotel (45)
6 Montague Street, WCI ☎ 0171-323 1717 ➡ 0171-636 6498

🔵 *Russell Square* **27 rooms** ●●● 📋 *free to residents* 🔲 📟 ⓞ 📺 📶 ✖ ✳ 🌿

Located in an 18th-century building in the heart of Bloomsbury, traditionally London's literary district, this hotel is decorated in the style of the turn of the century with antique furniture and old paintings, giving it something of the atmosphere of a private club. The entrance hall is delightful and there is access to a walled garden. The library is also something of a feature. This charming hotel holds to the belief that comfort is more important than glamor.

Montague Park Hotel (46)
15 Montague Street, WCI ☎ 0171-637 1001 ➡ 0171-637 2516

🔵 *Russell Square* 🅿 **105 rooms** ●●●● *4 suites £260* 📋 *£8* 🔲 ⓞ 📺 📶 🍴
Bistro 📶 ⊠ ✳ ✖ 🌿

Situated close to the British Museum, the Montague attracts more of a business clientele than its neighbor, Blooms. Following renovation work the traditional rooms are very comfortable, yet retain a quaint air. On the first floor are a bar and a charming restaurant. Doors open onto to a small terrace at the back of the hotel.

➥ 102 ■
Where to
shop ➥ 140

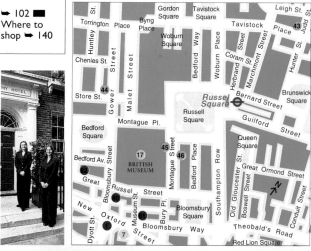

44

43   43

44

45

In the area

Predominantly residential, Marylebone has plenty of good shopping along Marylebone High Street and in the charming little streets around Baker Street. Major sightseeing attractions include Madame Tussauds. ■ Where to eat ➡ 74 ■ What to see ➡ 116 ➡ 118

Where to stay

Dorset Square Hotel (47)
39–40 Dorset Square, NW1 ☎ 0171-723 7874 ➡ 0171-724 3328

⊖ *Marble Arch* 🅿 **35 rooms** ●●●● *2 suites £205* 🖳 *£9.50* ▢ Ⓞ ▣ 📷 📠
🔲 *The Potting Shed* 🍸 ⚅ ✗ ✚ ♒

Dorset Square Hotel is the first of Tim and Kit Kemp's hotels that have set the standard for the English country-house style that has become so popular in London. Two Regency houses provide the setting for Kit Kemp's elegant touch, using strong colors, plenty of floral decorations, oil paintings, rich fabrics, antiques throughout (such as the 19th-century roll-top desk and antiques cabinet holding an honesty bar in the lounge) and luxurious furnishings. Some rooms have large four-poster beds and overlook the private garden square, the site of the original Lords cricket ground ➡ 134. The Potting Shed restaurant is charming, the bar an ideal place to relax and have a drink.

Durrants Hotel (48)
George Street, W1H ☎ 0171-935 8131 ➡ 0171-487 3510

⊖ *Bond Street, Baker Street* 🅿 **93 rooms** ●● *3 suites £205* 🖳 *£6.25* ▢ Ⓞ
📠 ▥ 🔲 *Durrants Restaurant* 🍸 *George Bar* ⚅ ✚

A long, four-story building, Durrants appears to belong to a past age of hotel keeping. First opened in 1790, it has been owned and managed by the Miller family since 1921 and still offers an old-fashioned, pleasant environment in a traditional setting. Wood paneled walls, leather banquettes in the restaurant, oil paintings and pretty, classic style in the bedrooms along with good, occasionally formal service, create a hotel where the guest is made to feel at ease and relaxed. A firm favorite with its many regulars.

The Leonard (49)
15 Seymour Street, W1H ☎ 0171-935 2010 ➡ 0171-935 6700

⊖ *Marble Arch* 🅿 **6 rooms** ●●●● *20 suites £311* 🖳 *£9.50* ▢ Ⓞ ▣ 📷 ▥
🔲 ▥ 🔲 🍸 🖳 ✗ ✚

Since opening in 1996, The Leonard has won numerous awards for its delightful decor and its exemplary, friendly service. Overseen by a genial young manager who knows the guests by name, the English town-house style of decor – good, bold color schemes, comfortable furniture, antiques, flowers and objets d'art – is predominant throughout. Four excellent and spacious suites occupy the upper floor with larger than usual drawing rooms; the first-floor lounge and Morning Room are perfect places for laden shoppers to stop and refuel with a drink or a snack.

Not forgetting

■ **The Landmark London (50)** 222 Marylebone Road, NW1
☎ 0171-631 8000 ➡ 0171-631 8033 ●●●●●

■ Where to shop ➡ 138

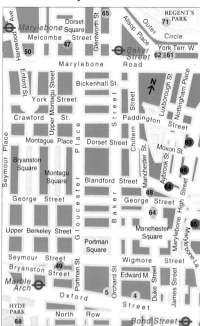

The George Bar in Durrants Hotel (above) is very popular. The atmosphere is more that of an old family home than a hotel.

In the area

One of London's most charming and fashionable districts, with small streets full of local stores and restaurants, and Portobello Antiques Market to attract the crowds. ■ Where to eat ➡ 64 ➡ 66 ■ After dark ➡ 84 ■ What to see ➡ 118 ■ Where to shop ➡ 158 ➡ 160

Where to stay

Portobello Hotel (51)
22 Stanley Gardens, W11 ☎ 0171-727 2777 ➡ 0171-792 9641

⊖ Notting Hill Gate **19 rooms** ●●● 3 suites £220 🎫 free to residents ▢ 🛈 🗗 📖 🛗 🍴 📺 ✂

Looking out onto a private garden and conveniently near Portobello Antiques Market, this small hotel was one of the first, idiosyncratic, London town-house hotels. It offers a variety of room sizes and decoration; the room with the Victorian bath virtually next to the bed might not appeal to the executive used to a modern hotel chain, but that is exactly the point here. A touch of the bohemian is what the Portobello is all about.

The Halcyon Hotel (52)
81 Holland Park, W11 ☎ 0171-727 7288 ➡ 0171-229 8516

⊖ Holland Park **25 rooms** ●●● 18 suites £295 🎫 £11 ▢ 🛈 🖥 📺 🗗 🛗 📖 🍴 The Room at the Halcyon ➡ 64 🍷 🍽 🗡 ✚ ★ ✂ @ 100712.2063@compuserve.com

It's easy to miss The Halcyon, two pink-washed houses on the corner of Holland Park and Addison Road with a discreet wrought-iron and glass canopied entrance. Yet this is characteristic of this elegant hotel, a well-kept secret which blends perfectly into the leafy, residential area and which attracts many locals to its bar and restaurant. Bedrooms are sumptuous, with rich furnishings and antiques, canopied beds and luxurious bathrooms; those overlooking gardens and tennis courts emphasize the rural character of this district of London.

The Hempel (53)
17 Craven Hill Gardens, W2 ☎ 0171-298 9000 ➡ 0171-402 4666

⊖ Lancaster Gate, Bayswater, Paddington **50 rooms** ●●●●● 🎫 £13.75 ▢ 🛈 🗗 📖 🛗 🍴 The I Thai 🍷 🍽 🗡 ✚ ★

A luxurious hotel rivaled only by Blakes Hotel ➡ 32, in South Kensington, the interior decor of which was also chosen by Anouska Hempel, owner of both hotels. Here the imaginative Hempel has cultivated minimalist chic along with high-tech comfort to the extent that mobile phones are provided to all guests. Each of the bedrooms and bathrooms are individually decorated in different styles. In one bedroom the bed is even suspended from the ceiling, as if in a lion's cage. The decor throughout is ultra-modern – black marble, wood and slate. The bar and restaurant of the Hempel are equally modern in style. The charming and friendly staff are all elegantly dressed in sophisticated, modern uniforms designed by the owner herself.

Not forgetting

■ **Abbey Court (54)** 20 Pembridge Gardens, W2 ☎ 0171-221 7518 ➡ 0171-792 0858 ●●●

Service charges

Many restaurants in central London add a 'service charge' to the check, usually 10 to 15%. This is increasingly replacing the custom of tipping waiting staff.

➡ Where to eat

Theater menus

Some restaurants offer special 'theater menus' (up to 7.30pm and sometimes after 9.30pm). These are less expensive than the regular menu.

Restaurants and areas

Different areas are well known for different types of restaurants: Soho for trendy restaurants, Covent Garden for vegetarian food, St James's, Mayfair and Knightsbridge for expensive restaurants, Chinatown for Chinese food, the East End for Indian food and along the Thames for restaurants with a view.

Fish & chips

For that great English classic try (eat in or take out):
Upper Street Fish Shop
324 Upper Street, N1
☎ 0171-359 1401

Modern British cuisine

Following the trend of some of London's top chefs such as Alastair Little ➡ 48 or Sally Clarke ➡ 64, the best London restaurants now offer Modern British cuisine. The food is a blend of traditional British fare (lamb, salmon); South East Asian flavorings (seaweed, spices); Mediterranean ingredients (basil, olives, sun-dried tomatoes). In London a new restaurant opens every day and another closes.

96
Restaurants

THE INSIDER'S FAVORITES

In the area

The area north of Long Acre – Neal Street, and the satellite streets around Seven Dials such as Earlham Street – is full of small fashion boutiques. Busy Neal's Yard has been the center of New Age London for decades, and has a collection of vegetarian cafés and take-outs.

Where to eat

Alfred (1)
245 Shaftesbury Avenue, W1 ☎ 0171-240 2566 ➡ 0171-497 0672

🔵 *Tottenham Court Road* **Traditional British cuisine** ●●● 🔲 🕐 *Mon.–Fri. noon–3.30pm, 6–11.30pm; Sat. 6–11.30pm* 🍸

Alfred is one of the new generation of restaurants that serves British food updated for the 1990s: traditional ingredients, cooked with flair. Wood pigeon salad is served with parsnip crisps and toasted rosemary bread, while puddings tend toward the sticky and filling. The carefully designed interior is reminiscent of the 1940s with its retro pastel colors and clever details.

World Food Café (2)
14 Neal's Yard (2nd floor), WC2 ☎ 0171-379 0298

🔵 *Covent Garden* **Vegetarian cuisine** ● 📁 🕐 *Mon.–Sat. noon–5pm*

The best of several vegetarian cafés in New Age Neal's Yard, with a fine view over the courtyard below. Meals are themed – Mexican tortillas, Sri Lankan *thali*, West African stews – and always fresh and appetizing. The staff are unfailingly pleasant and friendly, and the atmosphere is very mellow. Tapes of world music play in the background.

Belgo Centraal (3)
50 Earlham Street, WC2 ☎ 0171-813 2233 ➡ 0171-209 3213

🔵 *Covent Garden* **Belgian cuisine** ●● 🔲 🕐 *Mon.–Sat. noon–11.30pm; Sun. noon–8.30pm* 🍸 💠 *Belgo Noord, 72 Chalk Farm Road, NW1* ☎ 0171-267 0718

Entering these cellars by glass-walled walkway and industrial lift is like descending into the engine room of a ship, with steam, clanging metal and staff shouting orders. The low-ceilinged dining areas are patrolled by staff in monks' habits. Belgo's scores of wonderful Belgian beers from artisan brewers are well worth sampling. The mussels, fries and other simple Belgian dishes provide good accompaniment.

The Ivy (4)
1 West Street, WC2 ☎ 0171-836 4751 ➡ 0171-240 9550

🔵 *Leicester Square, Covent Garden* **Modern British cuisine** ●●● 🔲 🕐 *daily noon–3pm, 5.30pm–midnight* 🍸

The darling of London's media crowd, The Ivy manages to combine club-like intimacy with reliable good cooking. It's little surprise then that you need to book several days in advance, and that the staff will need your table all too soon for the next sitting. Simple classics such as Caesar salad, fine burgers, fish cakes and bang bang chicken – with a sprinkling of celebrities – usually make it worth the effort.

Not forgetting

■ **Food For Thought (5)** 31 Neal Street, WC2 ☎ 0171-836 0239 ●
Very busy vegetarian café; nourishing fast food at unbeatable prices, but very cramped.

A L F R E D

RESTAURANT · THE BASEMENT BAR · PAVEMENT CAFÉ

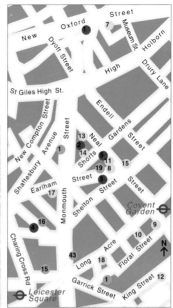

Neal's Yard is popular with the young and the
fashionable, and is packed with good vegetarian
cafés and trendy restaurants.

In the area

Covent Garden's piazza has more than its share of pricey, tourist-filled brasseries and cafés. However, some of the brasseries on Wellington Street are good value and pleasant places to eat. For something more luxurious, head south toward the Strand. ■ Where to stay ➡ 18

Where to eat

Bank (6)
1 Kingsway, WC2 ☎ 0171-379 9797 ➡ 0171-379 9014

☺ Holborn, Temple **Modern British cuisine** ●●● ▣ ◷ *Mon.–Sun. noon–3pm, 5.30–11.30pm* ▼ *Mon.–Sat. 11.30am–11.30pm; Sun. 11.30am–10.30pm* ◷ *Mon.–Fri. 7.30–10.30am*

A former bank building has been given a stunning makeover. The postmodern interior has a large bar area (where meals can also be ordered) by the entrance, but go past the exposed, glass-walled kitchen to the huge dining room beyond. Dishes from the lengthy menu are all excellent, from the simplest dishes – good fish and fries served with mushy peas – to exotic creations such as seared tuna sashimi.

Christopher's (7)
18 Wellington Street, WC2 ☎ 0171-240 4222 ➡ 0171-240 3357

☺ Covent Garden **American cuisine** ●●● ▣ ◷ *Mon.–Fri. noon–3pm, 6–11.45pm; Sat. 6–11.45pm* ▼ *Mon.–Sat. 11.30am–11pm; Sun. noon–3.30pm* ◷ *Sat. noon–4pm; Sun. noon–3.30pm*

The smart staff at the door alert you to the fact that this is not simply another American theme restaurant. On the first floor is a sports-style bar, but go up the baroque staircase to the sumptuous dining room. Most dishes are American classics, such as Maine lobster, steaks, crab cakes, clam chowder, or the best Caesar salad in the West End.

Rules (8)
35 Maiden Lane, WC2 ☎ 0171-836 5314 ➡ 0171-497 1081

☺ Covent Garden, Charing Cross **Traditional British cuisine** ●●● ▣ ◷ *Mon.–Sat. noon–midnight; Sun. noon–10.30pm*

Old Money from the Shires has pursued game here for nearly two centuries, making this London's oldest restaurant. The interior is richly decorated with prints and antlers. Although there are modern dishes such as risotto or salt cod, Rules is still best known for its grouse, wild duck, woodcock, rabbit and venison dishes.

Simpson's-in-the-Strand (9)
100 Strand, WC2 ☎ 0171-836 9112 0171-➡ 0171-836 1381

☺ Charing Cross **Traditional British cuisine** ●●● ▣ ▮▮ ◷ *Mon.–Fri. 7am–noon, noon–2.30pm, 5.30–11pm; Sat. noon–2.30pm, 5.30–11pm; Sun. noon–2.30pm, 6–9pm*

All that's best about traditional British food in a wonderful silver-service setting. Enjoy a huge fried breakfast, served with porridge and cereal or dine on roast beef with Yorkshire pudding. Desserts include favorites such as treacle roll with custard or bread-and-butter pudding. Dress code: jacket and tie, no sneakers or jeans.

Not forgetting

■ **Orso (10)** 27 Wellington Street, WC2 ☎ 0171-240 5269 ●●● *Imaginative Italian cuisine. Designer decor, showbiz clientele and rather noisy.*

■ After dark ➡ 90
■ What to see ➡
102 ■ Where to
shop ➡ 140 ➡ 160

Rules and Simpson's are
two traditional British
restaurants, serving food
that is reminiscent of
school dinners.

Soho, one of the most popular areas of London, has a vibrant and diverse street life, with a lively gay scene, pavement cafés, sex shows, fabric stores, and superb patisseries. ■ Where to stay ➡ 18 ■ After dark ➡ 90 ➡ 92 ➡ 94 ■ Where to shop ➡ 144 ➡ 160

Where to eat

Mezzo & Mezzonine (11)
100 Wardour Street, W1 ☎ 0171-314 4000 ➡ 0171-314 4040

🄴 *Tottenham Court Road, Leicester Square* ▯ 🕓 **Mezzo: Modern British cuisine** ●●●● *Mon.–Thur. noon–2.30pm, 6–11.30pm; Fri. noon–2.30pm, 6pm–12.30am; Sat. 6pm–12.30am; Sun. noon–2.30pm, 6–10.30pm* **Mezzonine: Oriental cuisine** ● *Mon.–Sat. noon–2.30pm, 7.30pm–12.30am; Sun. 7.30–11.30pm*

Sir Terence Conran's restaurant complex is one of the largest in Europe. Like many of Conran's creations, a place to see and be seen rather than a gastronomic treat. The upper floor is Mezzonine, an inexpensive canteen serving Pacific Rim dishes created by Australian chef John Torode; the Mezzo restaurant downstairs is expense-account territory with dishes in the Modern British convention. Reserve for downstairs, queue for upstairs.

Soho Soho (12)
11–13 Frith Street, W1 ☎ 0171-494 3491 ➡ 0171-437 3091

🄴 *Tottenham Court Road, Leicester Square* **French Mediterranean cuisine** ▯ 🕓 **Restaurant** ●●● *Mon.–Fri. noon–2.45pm, 6–11.45pm; Sat. 6–11.45pm* **Rotisserie** ●● *Mon.–Sat. noon–12.45am, Sun. noon–10.30pm* 🍸

On the first floor a noisy, hectic brasserie, packed with image-conscious local workers, often spills out on to the street, while the serene upper floor is more expensive and used by more senior members of the media brat pack. An attractive, fun place with a pleasant ambience. Although many of the Mediterranean-inspired dishes are no longer at the cutting edge of culinary fashion, meals here are reliable and satisfying. The bill is fair, though rarely low.

Sri Siam (13)
16 Old Compton Street, W1 ☎ 0171-434 3544 ➡ 0171-287 1311

🄴 *Tottenham Court Road, Leicester Square* **Thai cuisine** ●● ▯ 🕓 *Mon.–Sat. noon–3pm, 6–11.15pm; Sun 6–10.30pm*

The prettiest of the golden triangle of Thai restaurants around Old Compton Street presents dishes with typical Thai artistry. All the classics are there: *pad Thai* (stir-fried noodles), papaya salad, green curries, *tom yam* (hot and sour soup); plus a selection of vegetarian meals. Dishes can vary in quality, and the service can sometimes tend toward the abrupt.

Not forgetting

■ **Alastair Little (14)** 49 Frith Street, W1 ☎ 0171-734 5183 ●●● *Famous restaurant serving modern British food.* ■ **Bahn Thai (15)** 21a Frith Street, W1 ☎ 0171-437 8504 ●● *One of the best Thai restaurants in Soho, but the quality of food and the service are not always reliable.* ■ **Wagamama (16)** 10a Lexington Street, W1 ☎ 0171-292 0990 ● *Second branch of the popular Japanese ramen bar. Original is in Streatham Street, Bloomsbury ➡ 72.* ■ **Kulu Kulu (17)** 76 Brewer Street, W1 ☎ 0171-734 7316 ● *Japanese self-service sushi bar. Unusual, fast and inexpensive.*

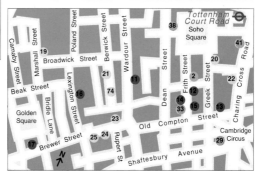

A spacious setting, dishes with a Southeast-Asian influence, and a kitchen visible from the dining room are some of the winning ingredients of many Soho restaurants.

In the area

In the last few years, many top chefs have moved from Hong Kong to London's Chinatown. As a result, some of the best Cantonese food in the world can be eaten here. Dim sum, tiny snacks served from lunchtime until around 5pm, are a good way to explore the food. Get

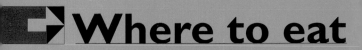

➡ Where to eat

Harbour City (18)
46 Gerrard Street, W1 ☎ 0171-439 7859 ➡ 0171-734 7745

🔵 *Leicester Square, Piccadilly Circus* **Chinese cuisine** ●● ▣ 🕐 *Mon.–Sat. noon–11.30pm; Sun. 11am–11pm*

Classic steamed dim sum dishes here include *char sui bun* (barbecued pork inside a steamed rice flour dumpling), and *cheung fun* (a type of pasta tube filled with pork or beef). Fried dishes include roast pork buns in a light pastry case.

Tokyo Diner (19)
2 Newport Place, WC2 ☎ 0171-439 287 8777 ➡ 0171-434 1415

🔵 *Leicester Square* **Japanese cuisine** ● 🗐 🕐 *daily noon–midnight*

The Japanese exterior is that of a diner in Tokyo. The illustrated menu is easy to understand, most meals are served in attractive bento boxes, and there is a Japanese-style no-tipping policy.

Golden Dragon (20)
28–29 Gerrard Street, W1 ☎ 0171-734 1073

🔵 *Leicester Square, Piccadilly Circus* **Chinese cuisine** ●● ▣ 🕐 *Mon.–Fri. noon–11.30pm; Sat. noon–midnight; Sun. 11am–11pm*

Superb dim sum is the attraction here. There are two main styles of dim sum, steamed and deep-fried. Order around two-thirds steamed dishes, one-third fried dishes. Dishes usually arrive in sets of three pieces, and cost under £2. A dozen dishes make a large meal for three people.

18

there early and order several dishes to share. ■ After dark ➡ 82 ➡ 84 ➡ 94 ■ What to see ➡ 104

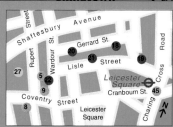

Fung Shing (21)
15 Lisle Street, WC2 ☎ 0171-437 1539 ➡ 0171-734 0284

🔵 *Leicester Square, Piccadilly Circus* **Chinese cuisine** ●●● ▣ 🕐 *daily noon–11.30pm*

A sleek new look has brought one of Chinatown's most respected restaurants into the 1990s. Dim sum is not served, but there are plenty of real Chinese dishes, such as steamed eel with black bean sauce, or salt-baked chicken.

Misato (22)
11 Wardour Street, W1 ☎ 0171-734 0808

🔵 *Leicester Square, Piccadilly Circus* **Japanese cuisine** ● ▣ 🕐 *daily noon–3pm, 6–10.30pm*

One of a new wave of budget Japanese diners in Chinatown, remarkable for the low prices and huge portions of simple dishes such as *katsu* curry (pork or chicken, deep-fried and served with curry and rice) or tempura (fish, shellfish or vegetables in batter).

Chinatown is also famous for its various stores – the perfect place to find all sorts of Chinese groceries and other products.

51

In the area

Leicester Square and Piccadilly Circus are in the very heart of London, and consequently packed with Londoners and visitors alike. Fast-food chains and expensive cafés predominate, but there are several excellent places to eat if you know where to look. ■ Where to stay ➡ 20

Where to eat

Al Waha (23)
20 Shaftesbury Avenue, W1 ☎ 0171-437 0411 ➡ 0171-437 0533

🔵 *Piccadilly Circus* **Lebanese cuisine** ●● ▣ 🕐 *Oct.–May: daily 11am–11.45pm; June–Sep.: daily 11–3am*

Al Waha serves authentic Lebanese dishes in a smart setting close to Piccadilly Circus. The staff are charming and eager to help you choose from the long list of meze dishes and chargrilled meat dishes. There is a minimum charge of £12 per head. It is advisable to book in advance.

L'Odéon (24)
65 Regent Street, W1 ☎ 0171-287 1400 ➡ 0171-287 1300

🔵 *Piccadilly Circus* **French cuisine** ●●●● ▣ 🕐 *Mon.–Fri. noon–3pm, 3.30–11.30pm; Sat. 5.30–11.30pm; Sun. 11.30am–4pm* 🍸

A large and stylishly-designed restaurant which manages to retain a friendly rather than frenetic feel. Bruno Loubet's cooking is modern and adventurous, but made with classical techniques – duck confit is glazed with honey and vinegar, served with stir-fried cabbages and roast vegetable purée. The set menus are excellent value. Reservations are essential here.

Criterion (25)
224 Piccadilly, W1 ☎ 0171-930 0488 ➡ 0171-930 8380

🔵 *Piccadilly Circus* **French cuisine** ●●● ▣ 🕐 *Mon.–Sat. noon–2.30pm, 6pm–midnight; Sun. noon–4pm, 6–10.30pm* 🍸

This is part of chef Marco Pierre White's fast-expanding empire, though he is only a consultant here. The best thing about the Criterion is the room itself, with its neo-Byzantine mosaic ceiling, long drapes and soft, romantic lighting. Not much MPW magic is apparent in the modern cooking, though it's perfectly competent. Service is briskly professional, but impersonal.

Café Fish (26)
39 Panton Street, SW1 ☎ 0171-930 3999 ➡ 0171-839 4880

🔵 *Piccadilly Circus* **Fish and seafood** ●● ▣ 🕐 *Mon.–Fri. noon–3pm, 5.45–11.30pm; Sat. 5.45–11.30pm* 🍸 🕐 *Mon.–Sat. 11.30am–11.30pm*

Panton Street is home to several cafés and budget restaurants, but Café Fish is the smart, mid-priced neighbor. The first floor is the restaurant, the basement a wine bar; you can eat in both. The cooking is to a good standard and the prices reasonable. It's always busy, so it's best to reserve or arrive early.

Not forgetting

■ **The Oak Room (27)** Meridien Piccadilly Hotel, 21 Piccadilly Circus, W1 ☎ 0171-437 0202 ●●●●● *London cuisine's enfant terrible, Marco Pierre White (and one of just two 3-star Michelin chefs) has decamped from the Hyde Park Hotel to the Oak Room at the Meridien. Worth following.*

■ After dark ➡ 84 ➡ 86 ■ What to see ➡ 104 ■ Where to shop ➡ 146 ➡ 148 ➡ 150

BURLINGTON HOUSE

Glasshouse St.
Denman St.
The Quadrant
Shaftesbury Ave.
Sackville St.
Piccadilly
Piccadilly Circus
Coventry St.
Regent St.
Jermyn Street
St James's Street
St James's Square
Haymarket
Rupert Street
Panton St.
Piccadilly Circus

25 24 27 33 24 28 23 27
45 46 34 29 17 8
8 35 38 36 5

24

24

26

25

23

26

25

23

The quality stores of Jermyn Street and the gentlemen's clubs of St James's may seemingly belong to a bygone age, but the restaurants to the south of Piccadilly are surprisingly modern. Beware, however, the prices are high. ■ Where to stay ➡ 20 ■ What to see ➡ 104 ➡ 118

 # Where to eat

Quaglino's (28)
16 Bury Street, SW1 ☎ 0171-930 6767 ➡ 0171-839 2866

🟢 *Green Park* **Modern British cuisine** ●●● ▭ 🕐 *Mon.–Thur., Sun. noon–2.45pm, 5.30–11.20pm; Fri., Sat. noon–3pm, 5.30pm–12.30am* 🍸 *Mon.–Thur. noon–1am; Fri., Sat. noon–2am; Sun. 5.30–11pm*

This was Terence Conran's flagship until he opened Mezzo ➡ 48, and although the novelty has worn off, it's still a stunning spectacle to enter this theatrically-designed restaurant down the sweeping staircase. The Conran attention to design detail is evident, though the food and portion sizes can sometimes disappoint. Reserve well in advance.

Matsuri (29)
15 Bury Street, SW1 ☎ 0171-839 1101 ➡ 0171-930 7010

🟢 *Green Park* **Japanese cuisine** ●●●● ▭ 🕐 *Mon.–Sat. noon–2.30pm, 6–10pm*

One of several upper echelon Japanese restaurants near the Japanese Embassy and business district. Matsuri offers sublime sushi, superb value set lunches, *teppan* tables (food is cooked before you on steel hotplates sunk into the table), and private tatami rooms (rush mat flooring). The presentation is flawless and the service impeccable.

The Avenue (30)
7–9 St James's Street, SW1 ☎ 0171-321 2111 ➡ 0171-321 2500

🟢 *Green Park* **Traditional British cuisine** ●●●● ▭ 🕐 *Mon.–Thur. noon–3pm, 5.45pm–midnight; Fri.–Sat. noon–3pm, 5.45pm–12.30am; Sun. noon–3pm, 6.45–10pm* 🍸

By the entrance, surreal art-school videos play on huge television screens; a long bar disappears into infinity. The main restaurant is vast and brightly lit. The cooking is fashionably European with pan-tropic touches: oxtail soup with horseradish dumplings, seared tuna with noodles.

L'Oranger (31)
5 St James's Street, SW1 ☎ 0171-839 3774 ➡ 0171-839 4330

🟢 *Green Park, Piccadilly Circus* **French nouvelle cuisine** ●●● ▭ 🕐 *Mon.–Sat. noon–3pm, 6–11pm; Sun. 6–10.30pm*

The oak paneling can give a first impression of a gentleman's club, but the atrium-roofed dining room is light and pleasant. The cooking is some of the best in London. A starter might include ravioli of salmon with crab jus; main courses could be panaché of fish with tagliatelle, or shin of beef braised in red wine with garlic and herbs.

Not forgetting
■ **Le Caprice (32)** Arlington House, Arlington Street, SW1 ☎ 0171-629 2239 ●●● *Modern British cuisine. Sunday brunch noon–3.30pm.*
■ **Suntory (33)** 72–73 St James's Street, SW1 ☎ 0171-409 0201 ●●●●● *Fabulous Japanese restaurant, despite the exorbitant prices.*

■ Where to shop
➡ 148 ➡ 150

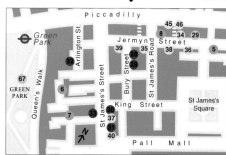

The largest restaurant area in London, The Avenue is a vast white space, lined with mirrors. The interior design was by Rick Mather.

30

31

28

31

31

29

Proximity to some of the best clothes shopping in the West End has given rise to some expensive, very stylish Modern British restaurants in this area. ■ Where to stay ➡ 24 ■ After dark ➡ 92 ■ What to see ➡ 104 ■ Where to shop ➡ 150 ➡ 152

Where to eat

Sotheby's Café (34)
34–35 New Bond Street, W1 ☎ 0171-408 5077 ➡ 0171-408 5920

🚇 Oxford Circus, Bond Street **Modern British cuisine** ●● ▣ 🕐 *Mon.–Fri. noon–2.30pm, 2.30–5pm (afternoon tea); Sun. noon–3.30pm* 🍸 🍴 *Mon.–Fri. 9.30am–noon*

Tucked away inside Britain's best-known auction house is a small, tastefully decorated café serving tasty fare suitable for fortifying the most discerning wheeler-dealers. Good quality British ingredients feature in dishes such as the salad of dandelions, lardons and quail's eggs, or the lobster club sandwich. A perfect place to stop for afternoon tea, for an impromptu celebration or a working lunch.

The Square (35)
6–10 Bruton Street, W1 ☎ 0171-495 7100 ➡ 0171-495 7150

🚇 Bond Street, Green Park **Modern British cuisine** ●●●● ▣ 🕐 *Mon.–Fri. noon–3pm, 6–11.45pm; Sat.–Sun. 6–11.45pm* 🍸

The Square relocated north of Piccadilly early in 1997, but retains the same accomplished chef (Phillip Howard) and the same management team. Expect to see the same elegant design that was once a feature of the King Street location, and to enjoy well-drilled service and high-quality imaginative cooking.

Nicole's (36)
158 New Bond Street, W1 ☎ 0171-499 8408 ➡ 0171-409 0381

🚇 Green Park **Modern British cuisine** ●●● ▣ 🕐 *Mon.–Fri. noon–5.30pm, 6.30–10.45pm; Sat. noon–5.30pm* 🍸 *Mon.–Sat. 11.30am–5.30pm* 🍴 *Mon.–Sat. 10am–11.30pm*

This small basement restaurant of the Nicole Farhi store serves excellent food for less than the price of a bauble upstairs. Those who enjoy shopping also need to eat – flagging shoppers can stop here at any time of day to rest and recharge, for breakfast, lunch, afternoon tea or dinner. The grilled, marinated vegetables are a succulent and wise choice if you're feeling conscious of your waistline, but more substantial fare includes dishes such as grilled lamb chump.

Coast (37)
26b Albemarle Street, W1 ☎ 0171-495 5999 ➡ 0171-495 2999

🚇 Green Park **Modern British cuisine** ●●● ▣ 🕐 *Mon.–Fri. noon–3pm, 6pm–midnight; Sat. 6pm–midnight; Sun. 6–10.30pm* 🍴 *Sat.–Sun. noon–3.30pm*

The tongue-in-cheek architecture and design owes as much to science fiction as it does to modernism, with curious moving 'art' and a strangely shaped white basement. Stephen Terry's cooking combines ingredients in unlikely ways, but the dishes are usually successful – venison with celeriac risotto and chocolate sauce, beetroot risotto with rocket, a dessert of vanilla cream with glazed tomato are all much better than they sound.

Anyone who has ever played the UK version of Monopoly knows that Mayfair is one of London's choicest districts. Park Lane is home to several of London's best hotel restaurants with no expense spared. There are cheaper bistros and wine bars to be found in the Shepherd

Where to eat

Connaught Restaurant & Grill (38)
16 Carlos Place, W1 ☎ 0171-499 7070 ➡ 0171-495 3262

🟢 *Green Park, Bond Street* **Gastronomic** ●●●●● ▢ 🕙 *daily 12.30–2.30pm, 6.30–10.45pm* 🍴 *Mon.–Sat. 11am–3pm, 5.30–11pm; Sun. noon–2.30pm, 7–10pm* 🍽 *daily 7.30–10am*

There are two stately, aristocratic restaurants in the Connaught – the large, wood-paneled Restaurant, and the smaller, gilded Grill. The staff look as if they are from a long line of specially-raised servants, and the Franglais menu too hails from another age with its avocado cocktails and steaks Diane. The place may be an anachronism, but neither food nor service can be faulted.

Dorchester Grill Room (39)
54 Park Lane, W1 ☎ 0171-317 6336 ➡ 0171-495 7342

🟢 *Hyde Park Corner* **Traditional British cuisine** ●●●● ▢ 🕙 *Mon.–Sat. 12.30–2.30pm, 6–11pm; Sun. 12.30–2.30pm, 7–10.30pm* 🍴 *Mon.–Sat. 11am–11pm; Sun. noon–10.30pm* 🍽 *Mon.–Sat. 7–10.30am; Sun. 7.30–11am*

This extraordinary room looks as if it belongs in a castle, with its gold and rust ornate ceiling, red leather chairs and plush sofas. The chef, Willi Elsener, uses local produce, but cooks both traditional and modern dishes. Morecambe Bay potted shrimps are on the menu, as are ginger crab cakes and duck and lentil cream soup. Superb set-priced menus keep the potentially enormous cost of eating here within reasonable bounds.

Tamarind (40)
20 Queen Street, W1 ☎ 0171-629 3561 ➡ 0171-499 5034

🟢 *Green Park* **Indian cuisine** ●●●● ▢ 🕙 *Mon.–Fri., Sun. noon–3pm, 6–11.30pm; Sat. 6–11.30pm* 🍴

Tamarind is probably the finest North Indian restaurant in the UK, with no expense spared on ingredients or getting the best chefs from Delhi. Since the restaurant opened in 1996, the dishes have evolved beyond their North Indian roots, and are reassuringly health-conscious with restrained use of oil and animal fats. The basement interior is exquisitely designed with hard gilded surfaces and subtle lighting.

Not forgetting

■ **Le Gavroche (41)** 43 Upper Brook Street, W1 ☎ 0171-408 0881 ●●●●● *Restaurant run by father and son Albert and Michel Roux and with a reputation dating back to 1967. Elegant and original haute cuisine. Friendly staff.* ■ **Chez Nico at Ninety Park Lane (42)** 90 Park Lane, W1 ☎ 0171-409 1290 ●●●●● *The chef Nico Ladenis offers the best of haute cuisine, Michelin three stars.* ■ **The Oriental (43)** The Dorchester Hotel, 53 Park Lane, W1 ☎ 0171-317 6328 ●●●●● *The best Chinese in London, at a price.* ■ **The Greenhouse (44)** 27a Hay's Mews, W1 ☎ 0171-499 3331 ●●● *Traditional British cuisine.* ■ **The Four Seasons (45)** Hamilton Place, W1 ☎ 0171-499 0888 ●●●● *Superb restaurant in the hotel of the same name* ➡ *24.*

Market area. ■ Where to stay
➡ 22 ➡ 24 ■ What to see
➡ 118 ■ Where to shop ➡
152

43

43

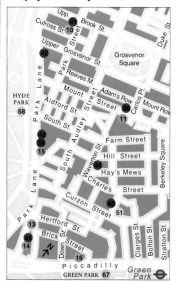

45

43

39

41

44

In the area

Everyone knows that Knightsbridge is exorbitant – it boasts London's largest parks, expensive cars, the most elegant shoes and some of the best restaurants. ■ Where to stay ➡ 28 ➡ 30 ■ After dark ➡ 92 ■ What to see ➡ 110 ➡ 118 ■ Where to shop ➡ 138 ➡ 154

➡ Where to eat

The Restaurant on the Park (46)
Mandarin Oriental Hyde Park, 66 Knightsbridge, SW1
☎ 0171-235 2000 ➡ 0171-235 4552

🔵 *Knightsbridge* **Gastronomic** ●● ▢ 🕐 *Mon.–Fri. noon–2.15pm, 7–11.15pm; Sat. 7–11.15pm*

David Nichols was chef at the Ritz for many years, and since September 1997, this first class chef has been in residence at the Mandarin, where he creates a delicious variety of dishes on the theme of foie gras. Set menus from £29.

Vong (47)
Berkeley Hotel, Wilton Place, SW1
☎ 0171-235 1010 ➡ 0171-235 1011

🔵 *Knightsbridge* **Thai cuisine** ●●● ▢ 🕐 *Mon.–Sat. noon–2.30pm, 6–11.30pm; Sun. 6–10pm*

Thai food with a twist, borrowing from many other cuisines. The rich, international jet-set clientele must wonder which continent they're on when they're served dishes like sautéed foie gras with ginger and mango, or sea bass in a sweet and sour mushroom broth.

Fifth Floor at Harvey Nichols (48)
Knightsbridge SW1 ☎ 0171-235 5250 ➡ 0171-823 2207

🔵 *Knightsbridge* **Modern British cuisine** ●●● ▢ 🕐 *Mon.–Fri. noon–3pm, 6.30–10.30pm; Sat. noon–3.30pm, 6.30–10.30pm; Sun. noon–3.30pm* 🍸

Harvey Nick's Fifth Floor houses a superb delicatessen, café-bar and restaurant. The bar is a favorite haunt for local Sloanes, but the restaurant is a relative haven of calm for hungry shoppers.

Salloos (49)
62–64 Kinnerton Street, SW1 ☎ 0171-235 4444 ➡ 0171-259 5703

🔵 *Knightsbridge* **Pakistani cuisine** ●●●● ▢ 🕐 *Mon.–Sat. noon–2.30pm, 7–11.15pm*

The most expensive Pakistani restaurant in London is also the best, with bland but sumptuous surroundings in a quiet mews street. Lamb and chicken are the main specialties, roasted in the tandoor (clay oven), grilled or karahi-fried (in an Indian wok). The breads and rice are also superb.

Not forgetting

■ **The Halkin (50)** 5–6 Halkin Street, SW1 ☎ 0171-333 1234 ●●●● *Hotel restaurant, Italian gastronomic.* ➡ 28. ■ **The Capital (51)** 22 Basil Street, SW3 ☎ 0171-589 5171 ●●●●● *Hotel gastronomic.* ➡ 30. ■ **Le Metro (51 on map)** 28 Basil Street, SW3 ☎ 0171-823 7826 ➡ 0171-823 7826 ●● *Modern British cuisine. Stop for a light breakfast, morning coffee, afternoon tea or lunch and dinner. Excellent value in this expensive area of town.* ■ **Emporio Armani Express (52)** 191 Brompton Road, SW3 ☎ 0171-823 8818 ●● *In-store Italian restaurant.* ■ **Zafferano (53)** 15 Lowndes Street, SW1 ☎ 0171-235 5800 ●●● *Italian cuisine.*

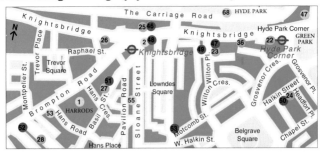

47

46

48

51

47

50

49

In the area

Brompton Road is home to the Conran Shop, Joseph and several other top fashion stores. Old Money mingles with New around Sloane Avenue, Draycott Avenue and Walton Street, resulting in a diverse and interesting range of places to eat and drink. ■ Where to stay ➡ 32 ■ What to

 # Where to eat

The Collection (54)
264 Brompton Road, SW3 ☎ 0171-225 1212 ➡ 0171-225 1050

❸ *South Kensington* **Pacific Rim and Mediterranean** ●●● ▣ ◔ *Mon.–Sat. noon–3pm, 7–11.30pm* ▣ *Mon.–Sat. noon–11pm*

This former fashion warehouse is reached by negotiating remote-controlled bouncers and a long, glass-floored tunnel. The ground floor is a cavernous bar and bistro, bustling with local young trendies, but make reservations for the more tranquil restaurant on the mezzonine floor where some brilliantly creative dishes are served. Some of the mediterranean dishes can sometimes be disappointing, but the Pacific Rim assemblies, such as seared tuna sashimi with soy, *daikon* and shiitake mushrooms, are particularly recommended.

Hilaire (55)
68 Old Brompton Road, SW7 ☎ 0171-584 8993 ➡ 0171-581 2949

❸ *South Kensington* **Modern British cuisine** ●●● ▣ ◔ *Mon.–Fri. 12.30–2.30pm, 6.30–11.30pm; Sat. 6.30–11.30pm*

A delightful small, intimate restaurant which is attractively decorated in daffodil yellow with light wooden paneling and a huge, sweeping glass front. Welsh chef-patron Bryn Webb uses only the best produce in his cooking, favoring British ingredients wherever possible. The menu includes dishes such as oxtail meatballs served with mashed potato and a red wine sauce, grilled oysters served with laverbread (seaweed) and stilton. Service is friendly, and the wine list good but fairly expensive.

Bibendum (56)
Michelin House, 81 Fulham Road, SW3
☎ 0171-581 5817 ➡ 0171-823 7925

❸ *South Kensington* **Modern British cuisine** ●●●●● ▣ ◔ *Mon.–Fri. 12.30–2.30pm, 7–11.30pm; Sat. 12.30–3pm, 7–11.30pm; Sun. 12.30–3pm, 7–11.30pm* ▣ *daily noon–10.30pm*

This is one of the most expensive restaurants in London. Value-for-money may not be a strong point, but Bibendum is an impressive dining experience. The stained-glass ex-garage windows are foiled by a plain and demure interior, much more modest in design than other Conran restaurants. Chef Matthew Harris offers a range of delicious imaginative creations, but the service is occasionally less than perfect for the high prices charged. Reserve well in advance, or queue for the less expensive seafood bar downstairs.

Not forgetting

■ **Pizza Chelsea (57)** 93 Pelham Street, SW7 ☎ 0171-584 4788 ●
Very good pizza and very reasonably priced in an area that tends to be particularly expensive.
■ **Francofill (58)** 1 Old Brompton Road, SW7 ☎ 0171-584 0087 ● *Fast French food with simple dishes such as steak, fries, ragout, ratatouille and Tarte Tatin. Largely attracts a young, French-speaking crowd.*

see ➡ 114 ◼ Where to shop ➡ 154

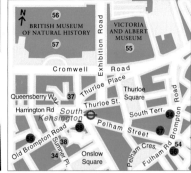

56

56

55

55

54

56

In the area

Kensington Church Street, famous for its antique shops, has a number of mid-range restaurants from the crest of the hill down toward Notting Hill Gate tube. This is the smart end of North Kensington, a world away from the Portobello Road side of Notting Hill Gate. ■ Where to stay

Where to eat

Kensington Place (59)
201–205 Kensington Church Street, W8
☎ 0171-727 3184 ➠ 0171-229 2025

◐ *Notting Hill Gate* **Modern British cuisine** ●●● ▣ ◷ *Mon.–Fri. noon–3pm, 6.30–11.45pm; Sat. noon–3.30pm, 6.30–11.45pm; Sun. noon–3.30pm, 6.30pm–10.15pm*

Before Bank, and before Fifth Floor, Harvey Nichols' Julyan Wickham designed this plate-glass-fronted canteen and defined the look for a whole generation of the capital's most fashionable restaurants. Its appearance is just as striking now as it was when the restaurant first opened, and the food remains as excellent as ever – plenty of fish and seafood, goat's cheese, lentils, polenta, pesto, tapenade, pine kernels and a whole host of other fashionable ingredients grilled, steamed and roasted for the mobile-phone carrying customers. The drawbacks are the fast turnaround (no possibility of a long leisurely lunch) and the noise level.

Clarke's (60)
124 Kensington Church Street, W8
☎ 0171-221 9225 ➠ 0171-229 4564

◐ *Notting Hill Gate* **Modern British cuisine** ●●●● ▣ ◷ *Mon.–Fri. 12.30–2pm, 7–11pm*

Sally Clarke (right) was, and still is, one of the pioneers of Modern British cookery. Her set menu meals offer a very limited choice, although you can telephone on the actual day to check what the daily menu contains. Only the freshest and best ingredients are used, and they are usually organic; perhaps a salad of pear, rocket and Parmesan shavings with crostini, followed by pigeon breasts chargrilled with red wine glaze and salad of cress and walnuts. The wine list, put together with as much thought as the food menu itself, offers a considered selection of good-quality California wines.

The Abingdon (61)
54 Abingdon Road, W8 ☎ 0171-937 3339 ➠ 0171-795 6388

◐ *High Street Kensington, Earl's Court* **French cuisine** ●● ▣ ◷ *Mon.–Sat. noon–2.30pm, 6.30–11pm; Sun. noon–3pm, 6.30–11.30pm* ▮ *Mon.–Sat. noon–11.30pm*

Located in a quiet, residential neighborhood full of little mews houses, this attractively designed bar and restaurant has a welcoming feel. The large bar with its comfortable sofas is a great place to meet for a drink. The restaurant has a different lunchtime menu each day. The chef (Brian Baker) specializes in straightforward French food – duck confit, pan-fried chicken breast, or poached cod with mussels, leeks and potatoes.

Not forgetting

■ **The Room at the Halcyon (62)** 129 Holland Park Avenue, W11 ☎ 0171-221 5411 ●●● *Gastronomic hotel-restaurant, next to the Halcyon Hotel* ➠ 40.

➡ 40 ■ What to see ➡ 118

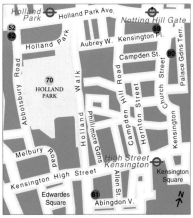

60

61

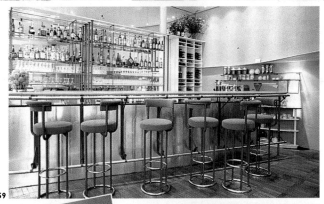

59

59

59

Queensway is the main area in Bayswater, with its late-night opening hours and constant bustle, but it's much more interesting to move along to the more colorful Westbourne Grove into the heart of Notting Hill.
■ Where to stay ➡ 40 ■ Where to shop ➡ 158 ➡ 160

Where to eat

The Sugar Club (63)
33a All Saints Road, W11 ☎ 0171-221 3844

◉ Westbourne Park **Global fusion, Pacific Rim cuisine** ●●● ▣ ◲ daily 12.30–3pm, 6.30–11pm

Not a salubrious area, but worth the trip for Peter Gordon's extraordinary cooking. He draws on his New Zealand heritage and his travels in Asia to pull off culinary wonders such as seared tuna on *soba* (buckwheat) noodles with *hijiki* seaweed, sesame and *wasabi* (Japanese 'mustard'), grilled kangaroo loin on cumin-butter roast parsnips with green beans and *harissa*, or grilled squid with cucumber, peppers and sweet potato chips.

The Cow Dining Room (64)
89 Westbourne Park Road, W2 ☎ 0171-221 0021

◉ Westbourne Park **Italian cuisine** ●● ▣ ◲ Mon.–Sat. 7–11.30pm; Sun. 12.30–3.30pm ☘ daily 11am–11pm (food 12.30–3.30pm, 6.30–11.30pm)

One of a growing breed of 'gastropubs' taking over Notting Hill and Westbourne Park. You can eat in the mock-Irish pub on the first floor, but for greater seclusion (and to escape from the local bohemians) the delightful dining room upstairs serves a good selection of Italianate dishes, such as risottos, lamb's sweetbreads served with pancetta, thyme and cream, or baked goat's cheese with tapenade toasts.

Orsino (65)
119 Portland Road, W11 ☎ 0171-221 3299 ➡ 0171-229 9414

◉ Holland Park **Italian cuisine** ●●● ▣ ◲ daily noon–11pm

A delightful peach- and terracotta-colored place which could be in Tuscany, except the portions there would be bigger. Not all the dishes are successful, some are a little crudely thrown together, but on the whole this a pleasant place to toy with some antipasti, pizzas, pasta dishes, or main courses such as roast sea bass with lime leaves and new potatoes. The wine list is good, but incomprehensible.

Royal China (66)
13 Queensway, W2 ☎ 0171-221 2535 ➡ 0171-221 2535

◉ Queensway, Bayswater **Chinese cuisine** ●● ▣ ◲ daily noon–11pm

The Kensington Gardens end of Queensway has a small cluster of the few really good Chinese restaurants outside Chinatown ➡ 50, and this in one of the best, serving superb dim sum until 5pm every day. Order a mixture of steamed and deep-fried dishes then sit back and appreciate the black lacquer, split-level interior.

Not forgetting

■ **192 Restaurant (67)** 192 Kensington Park Road, W11 ☎ 0171-229 0482 ●● *Modern British cuisine and one of the best wine lists in London and very fashionable.*

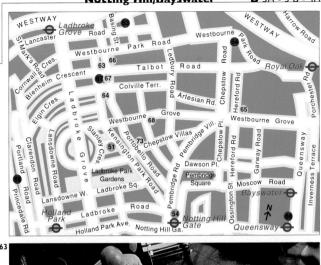

Like neighboring Fulham, this is a fashionable residential district with a good selection of mid-priced places to eat, plus a few stunningly good, if expensive, restaurants. ■ Where to stay ➠ 30 ■ After dark ➠ 82 ➠ 92 ■ Where to shop ➠ 156

Where to eat

Aubergine (68)
11 Park Walk, SW10 ☎ 0171-352 3449 ➠ 0171-351 1770

⊖ *South Kensington* **Gastronomic** ●●●●● ▭ ◐ *Mon.–Fri. 12.15–2pm, 7–10.30pm; Sat. 7–10.30pm*

This is the kind of restaurant you can take your parents to: unfailingly attentive Francophile staff, a chintzy but comfortable interior, and a low hubbub from the diners' conversations. Chef Gordon Ramsay's cooking is some of the best you'll find in the UK. Look out for dishes such as his 'cappuccinos', strongly flavored frothy ice-cream dishes; or the blanquette of turbot with ravioli of oyster, cucumber and caviar sauce. You will need to reserve several weeks in advance.

The Canteen (69)
Unit G4 Harbour Yard, Chelsea Harbour, SW10
☎ 0171-351 7330

⊖ *Fulham Broadway, Sloane Square* **French and Modern British cuisine** ●●● ▭ ◐ *Mon.–Thur. noon–3pm, 6.30–11pm; Fri.–Sat. noon–3pm, 6.30pm–midnight; Sun. noon–3pm*

Chelsea Harbour is a modern residential and shopping complex by the Thames, a throwback to Thatcherite architecture. The Canteen is the best thing about the area, with highly polished service, fine views over the pristine yachts in the harbor (if you are fortunate enough to manage to get a window seat), and superb cooking somewhere between French and Modern British cuisine.

Tante Claire (70)
68 Royal Hospital Road, SW3 ☎ 0171-352 6045 ➠ 0171-352 3257

⊖ *Sloane Square* **French cuisine** ●●●●● ▭ ◐ *Mon.–Fri. 12.30–2pm, 7–11pm*

Pierre Koffmann is not one of those celebrity chefs who spends more time on television or arranging franchises than he does in the kitchen. He has made it to the very top, and stayed there for two decades, by complete devotion to his cooking. The menu features Gascony dishes and ingredients such as venison, pigeon, duck, foie gras and rabbit, though his most famous dish is braised pig's trotters with morels. There is a minimum charge at dinner of £50 per person.

Not forgetting

■ **Fulham Road (71)** 257–259 Fulham Road, SW3 ☎ 0171-351 7823 ●●● *Modern British cuisine specialties: eggplant 'caponata' with tomato coulis, smoked haddock risotto with cream, lamb served with tortellini with wild garlic, and a dessert of lemon soufflé.*
■ **Bluebird (72)** 350 King's Road, SW3 ☎ 0171-559 1000 ●●●● *Terence Conran's latest venture: a dining room that seats 240 people. A hundred or so cooks prepare European and Australian-inspired dishes.*
■ **Charco's (73)** 1 Bray Place, SW3 ☎ 0171-584 0765 ●● *Varied international cuisine. Good wine list. Excellent value for money.*

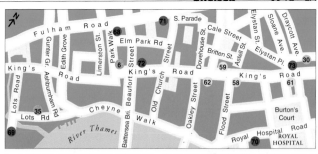

Gordon Ramsay, head chef at Aubergine, has published a book of his own recipes: *Passion for Flavour.*

Many restaurants in the city cater for business dining, which can curb creativity and opening hours – few places open late or at weekends. In contrast, Clerkenwell, north of Smithfield Meat Market, has a lively restaurant scene. ■ After dark ➡ 82 ➡ 86 ➡ 88 ■ What to see ➡ 100

 # Where to eat

Quality Chop House (74)
94 Farringdon Road, EC1 ☎ 0171-837 5093

⊖ *Farringdon* **Traditional British cuisine** ●● 📋 🕐 *Mon.–Fri. noon–3pm, 6.30–11.30pm; Sat. 6.30–11.30pm; Sun. noon–4pm, 7–11.30pm*

In Victorian times chop houses were places where workers could eat their fill of cheap fare. This beautiful interior of tiled floor, wooden tables and hard benches has been preserved and faithfully restored, while the food has been elevated and extended way beyond traditional British stodgy offerings with such dishes as salmon fishcakes and sorrel sauce, *bang bang* chicken or Argentinian corned beef hash with egg appearing on the menu.

St John (75)
26 St John Street, EC1 ☎ 0171-251 0848 ➡ 0171-251 4090

⊖ *Farringdon* **Traditional British cuisine** ●● ▢ 🕐 *Mon.–Fri. noon–3pm, 6–11.30pm; Sat. 6–11.30pm* 🍸 *Mon.–Sat. 11am–11pm; Sun. noon–3pm*

Unlike most restaurants which tend to offer dishes based on the more widely acceptable cuts of meat, Fergus Henderson's menu is almost entirely offal-based. Dishes include the likes of roast bone marrow and parsley salad, duck neck and gizzard terrine, and smoked eel, bacon and peas. Vegetables might include sprout tops, cob nuts and wet walnuts, or buttered sea kale. The restaurant is plain and simple in the extreme. Not for the squeamish.

Moshi, Moshi, Sushi (76)
Unit 24, Liverpool Street Station, Platform 1, EC2
☎ 0171-247 3227 ➡ 0171-247 3227

⊖ *Liverpool Street* **Sushi bar, Japanese cuisine** ● ▢ 🕐 *Mon.–Fri. 11.30am–9pm*

This glass-walled store overlooking the trains leaving Liverpool Street Station was the first sushi bar in Britain to use a *kaiten* (conveyor belt) to allow customers to inspect their sushi before helping themselves. This ingenious system, which is extremely common in Japan, is gradually growing in popularity in London. Quality of food is of a high standard.

Sri Thai (77)
Bucklersbury House, 3 Queen Victoria Street, EC4
☎ 0171-827 0202 ➡ 0171-827 0200

⊖ *Bank* **Thai cuisine** 🔳 ●● ▢ 🕐 *Mon.–Fri. 11.30am–8.30pm* 🍸 *Mon.–Fri. 11.30am–11pm* 🔼 *Sri Siam* ➡ 48

This delicious Thai restaurant pays particular attention to presentation. From the spacious, well-lit dining area to the dishes, decorated with sculpted vegetables, everything is esthetically pleasing. The Sri Thai starters, which consist of a selection of Thai specialties, is an excellent choice to whet your appetite. This restaurant has another outlet in the center of Soho: the Sri Siam.

The healthier approach to fast food

76

St. JOHN

75

75

76

71

Charlotte Street, the center of the media district, has several mid-priced restaurants and inexpensive cafés. The British Museum in Bloomsbury has good, inexpensive places to eat, but if you prefer to eat with Londoners try Wagamama or the Museum Street Café. ■ Where to

 # Where to eat

Interlude (78)
5 Charlotte Street, W1 ☎ 0171-637 0222 ➡ 0171-637 0224

◉ *Goodge Street, Tottenham Court Road* **French cuisine** ●●●● ▣ ◔ *Mon.– Fri. noon–2.30pm, 7–11pm; Sat. 7–11pm*

Formerly known as 'Interlude de Chavot', this establishment was renamed in 1997 by its new chef Anand Sastry. This small, quiet, chintzy restaurant is very simply decorated. The food is simply delicious – not overly garnished or showy, but revealing a deep understanding of flavor and texture. Try the rump of lamb, served with polenta and couscous, or osso bucco braised in Madeira and served with fresh pasta.

Chez Gérard (79)
8 Charlotte Street, W1 ☎ 0171-636 4975 ➡ 0171-637 4564

◉ *Goodge Street, Tottenham Court Road* **French cuisine** ●● ▣ ◔ *Mon.–Fri. noon–3pm, 6–11.30pm; Sat. 6–11.30pm; Sun. noon–3pm, 6–10.30pm*

A chic restaurant, painted magnolia but modernized with neat architectural detail and sharply-dressed waiting staff. The food is middle-of-the road French cooking, but done well; advertising executives pour in here for some of the finest steak and fries to be found in the center of town.

Wagamama (80)
4 Streatham Street, WC1 ☎ 0171-323 9223 ➡ 0171-323 9224

◉ *Tottenham Court Road* **Japanese noodle bar** ● ▣ ◔ *Mon.–Sat. noon–11pm; Sun. 12.30–10pm* 🔲 *Wagamama* ➡ 48

Close to the British Museum, this basement ramen bar usually has a fast-moving queue snaking up the stairs. This canteen, with its strikingly designed interior, is popular with a predominantly young clientele who don't mind the crush or the fast turnaround. Diners share benches at long wooden tables. The food combines Japanese and South-East Asian. No smoking.

Museum Street Café (81)
47 Museum Street, WC1 ☎ 0171-405 3211 ➡ 0171-405 3211

◉ *Holborn, Tottenham Court Road* **Modern British cuisine** ▱ ●● ▣ ◔ *Tue.–Fri. 12.30–2.30pm, 6.30–9.30pm*

A plain and simply decorated restaurant serving good quality meals. The menus are fixed price with a limited choice per course. Vegetarians fare well here – perhaps lentil, red wine and chestnut soup, followed by warm goat's cheese with sweet potatoes, courgettes and tomatoes – while meat-eaters have a choice of fish or chargrilled meats. Reservations are essential.

Not forgetting
■ **Malabar Junction (82)** 107 Great Russell Street, WC1
☎ 0171-580 5230 ● *Good Indian restaurant specializing in Southern Indian dishes.*

stay ➥ 36 ■ After dark ➥
92 ➥ 94 ■ What to see
➥ 102

80

79

79

wagamama
KAIZEN

81

81

82

In the area

Marylebone, a business district and also a relatively peaceful residential area, retains a slightly gentrified air. There is little of interest here for the visitor other than several small stores, Oxford Street (to the south) and Madame Tussaud's (to the north). ■ Where to stay ➡ 38 ■ After

Where to eat

Villandry Dining Room (83)
89 Marylebone High Street, W1
☎ 0171-224 3799 ➡ 0171-486 1370

🔵 *Baker Street* **French cuisine** ●● ▭ 🕐 *Mon.–Sat. 12.30–3pm* 😋 *Mon.–Sat. 8.30–11.30am* ⊞

At the front is a *traiteur* selling fine foods. Chosen ingredients are used in the French-style bistro at the rear. The charcuterie and selection of cheeses are excellent, and even salads and pasta dishes are prepared with gusto. The chairs wobble, the tables are too tightly packed and the service varies from brisk to brusque, but it is still a fun place to have lunch. A new branch is located in nearby Great Portland Street.

Stephen Bull (84)
5–7 Blandford Street, W1 ☎ 0171-486 9696 ➡ 0171-490 3128

🔵 *Baker Street, Bond Street* **Modern British cuisine** ●●● ▭ 🕐 *Mon.–Fri. 12.15–2.30pm, 6.30–10.30pm; Sat. 6.30–10.30pm* 🍴 *Stephen Bull's Bistro, 571 St John Street, EC1* ☎ *0171-490 1750*

Stephen Bull's has a clean and bright minimal look; warmth is added by the friendly front-of-house staff, who are predominantly French. The cooking is good with clear and distinct flavors in every dish. The twice-cooked goat's cheese soufflé, seared red mullet, and salted belly of pork with lentils, mushrooms and rosemary are seldom bettered. The puddings might include intensely-flavored raspberry and geranium crème brûlée, or a lime and white chocolate terrine with blackberries. The wine list is carefully chosen and reasonably priced. Food prices tend to be on the high side, but the quality and presentation are extremely good. Perfect for lunch after a morning in the Wallace Collection ➡ 116.

Union Café & Restaurant (85)
96 Marylebone Lane, W1 ☎ 0171-486 4860

🔵 *Bond Street* **Modern British cuisine** ●● ▭ 🕐 *Mon.–Sat. 12.30–3.30pm, 6.30–10.30pm* 😋 *Mon.–Sat. 9.30am–noon* 🍴 *Mon.–Sat. 6.30–10.30pm*

The plate-glass windows give a first impression of dining in an aquarium, but once inside diners seem happy to linger in this somewhat bare eating area. The café tables belie a kitchen which takes carefully-sourced ingredients and fastidiously prepares reasonably priced dishes. The food is not elaborate with the chargrill, the main source of heat, used to cook fish and vegetables. Couscous is served Moroccan-style with chickpeas and vegetables, peppers are roasted and served with mozzarella and pancetta on a pizza. Early closing Saturday and Sunday, but during the week it's busy at lunchtimes, quieter in the evenings, and perfect for a leisurely breakfast.

Not forgetting

■ **Patisserie Valérie at Maison Sagné (86)** 105 Marylebone High Street, W1 ☎ 0171-935 6240 ● *High-quality French patisserie, a perfect place for coffee, lunch or afternoon tea. Delicious pastries, tarts and cakes to eat in or take out. Other branches in Soho, Knightsbridge, Covent Garden and Portland Place.*

dark ➡ 88 ■ What to see ➡ 116

TISSERIE VALERIE

Typically French products have always been popular in London.

UNION

86

84

85

In the area

The South Bank Arts Centre – containing The People's Palace and several Aroma sandwich bars – and Waterloo Station dominate this area. A short walk east along the bank of the Thames takes you to Gabriel's Wharf – a craft market with several inexpensive brasseries – to the

Where to eat

The People's Palace (87)
Royal Festival Hall, 4th floor, South Bank Centre, SE1
☎ 0171-928 9999 ➡ 0171-928 2355

🅴 *Waterloo, Embankment* **Modern British cuisine** ●●● ⬛ 🕓 *daily noon–3pm, 5.30–11pm* 🍸 🌿

The river-facing restaurant on Level 3 was given a new lease of life in 1995 with complete refurbishment, new management, a team of staff who can handle everything from a swift drink to large parties with aplomb, and Modern British cooking which is completely up-to-date (beetroot tart tatin; risotto of roast pumpkin with macadamia nuts and sorrel), although portions are small, and prices are high. Ask for a riverside seat: the views over the Thames are magnificent.

Oxo Tower Restaurant & Brasserie (88)
Barge House Street, South Bank, SE1
☎ 0171-803 3888 ➡ 0171-803 3838

🅴 *Blackfriars, Waterloo* **Modern British cuisine** ⬛ 🕓 *Restaurant* ●●●● *Mon.–Sat. noon–3pm, 6–11pm; Sun. 11am–10pm* **Brasserie** ●●● *Mon.–Sat. 11am–11pm; Sun. 11am–10pm* 🍸 *daily 11am–10pm* 🌿

This landmark used to be the headquarters of a brand of stock cube, but was left derelict for many years. In autumn 1996 it was reopened by Harvey Nichols to great acclaim, with an elegant and rather expensive restaurant on the 9th floor, a brasserie (better value for money than the restaurant, if a little noisy) and a bar. The views through the glass-walled terrace across the river are impressive enough, but these are also combined with sleek design, smooth service and assured Modern British cooking. Reservations are essential for both lunchtime and evening.

Livebait (89)
43 The Cut, SE1 ☎ 0171-928 7211 ➡ 0171-928 5590

🅴 *Waterloo* **Fish and seafood** ●● ⬛ 🕓 *Mon.–Sat. noon–3pm, 5.30–11.30pm*

This delightful restaurant is a short walk from Waterloo Station, and close to the Old Vic and Young Vic theaters. It was once a Victorian pie and mash store, and the look has been carefully restored with wooden bench seating and tiled walls. Fresh fish and shellfish are displayed on an ice counter. The quality of the fish and seafood is superb, the dishes are cooked to perfection (the *plateau de fruits de mer* is particularly recommended), the staff friendly, and the prices are competitive.

Not forgetting

■ **The Fire Station (90)** 150 Waterloo Road, SE1 ☎ 0171-620 2226 ●●
Lively, noisy bar-restaurant in the former fire station in Waterloo station. The menu is made up of primarily Modern British dishes. A good place to go for a quick drink before catching a train. Fashionable, lively and perfect for a pre- or post-theater dinner.

impressive Oxo Tower.
- After dark ➡ 86 ➡ 88
- What to see ➡ 108

In the area

The London Docklands declined during the 1970s. Designer Terence Conran (together with the London Docklands Development Corporation) was the first, in the late 1980s, to capitalize on the superb riverside site of Shad Thames and the striking warehouse buildings;

Where to eat

Le Pont de la Tour (91)
36d Shad Thames, Butlers Wharf, SE1
☎ 0171-403 8403 ➟ 0171-403 0267

⊖ Tower Hill, London Bridge **French cuisine** ▯ ◷ **Restaurant** ●●●●● Mon.–Fri., Sun. noon–3pm, 6–11pm; Sat. 6–11.30pm **Bar & Grill** ●●● Mon.–Sat. 11.30am–11.30pm; Sun. noon–11pm

Terence Conran's most ambitious restaurant by Tower Bridge has an elegant and very stylish interior. The quality of the seafood is superb with a French accent to many of the dishes. The high prices guarantee that the adjoining bar, which also serves food, is always popular.

Butlers Wharf Chop House (92)
36e Shad Thames, Butlers Wharf, SE1
☎ 0171-403 3403 ➟ 0171-403 3414

⊖ Tower Hill, London Bridge **Traditional British cuisine** ▯ ◷ **Restaurant** ●●● Mon.–Fri. noon–3pm, 6–11pm; Sat. 6–11pm; Sun. noon–3pm **Bar** ●● Mon.–Sat. noon–3pm, 6–11pm; Sun. noon–3pm

The Chop House boasts a fresh, modern interior, almost Scandinavian in look, and the cooking is elevated far beyond the usual traditional English stodgy food. Jugged rabbit with lemon and sage dumplings, pork chops with apple sauce, and Cambridge burnt cream are all excellent.

Blueprint Café (93)
Design Museum, Shad Thames, Butlers Wharf, SE1 ☎ 0171-378 7031

⊖ Tower Hill, London Bridge **Modern British cuisine** ●●● ▯ ◷ Mon.–Sat. noon–3pm, 6.30–11pm; Sun. noon–3pm 🌿

Conran's Blueprint is less expensive and better value than the plusher 'Chop House' and 'Pont', with cooking in the current trend of the capital: roast artichoke and green bean salad, roast cod with fennel, courgettes and herbs, calves liver with potatoes, pancetta and balsamic vinegar. Modern interior and a view of the Thames.

Café Spice Namaste (94)
16 Prescot Street, E1 ☎ 0171-488 9242 ➟ 0171-488 9339

⊖ Tower Hill, Aldgate East **Indian cuisine** ●● ▯ ◷ Mon.–Fri. noon–3pm, 6.15–10.30pm; Sat. 6.30–10pm

To the north of Tower Bridge, a Victorian building provides the setting for the most innovative Indian restaurant in London. The lengthy menu is carefully chosen by chef, Cyrus Todiwala, who is very imaginative in his search for new dishes. The results are often out of this world. The Parsi and Goan dishes are always excellent.

Not forgetting

■ **Cantina del Ponte (95)** 36c Shad Thames, Butlers Wharf, SE1 ☎ 0171-378 7031 ●● *Italian cuisine in another of Terence Conran's eating houses.*
■ **Delfina Studio Café (96)** 50 Bermondsey Street, SE1 ☎ 0171-357 0244 ●● *Modern British cuisine. Light and airy, with temporary art exhibitions.*

he has made Shad Thames his own gastrodrome, and created several elegant restaurants.
■ What to see ➡ 98

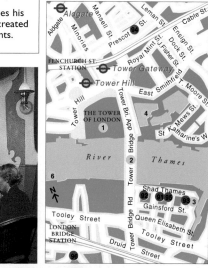

93

93
92

94

91

After dark

Half-Price Ticket Booth

Clock Tower Building, Leicester Square, WC2 🕐 *Mon.–Sat. noon–6.30pm*
Half-price theater tickets (cash only) for a wide selection of West End shows on the day of the performance.

If a show you wished to see is already sold out, try queuing for same day returns at the actual theater. Some theaters also have a policy of standby tickets that are only available on the day.

45

Nights out

THE INSIDER'S FAVORITES

Calendar of cultural events

Jan. International Festival of Mime ☎ 0171-637 5661

Feb.–Mar. Spring Loaded Festival *Place Theatre* ☎ 0171-387 0031

May–June Covent Garden Festival

May–Sep. Open Air Theatre *Regent's Park* ☎ 0171-935 5756

June–July City of London Festival *Barbican Centre* ☎ 0171-638 8891

July English Heritage Summer Music ☎ 0171-413 1443

July–Aug. Holland Park Opera ☎ 0171-602 7856

Jul.–Sep. The Proms ☎ 0171-765 5575 / 0171-589 8212

Sep.–Oct. Soho Jazz Festival *Knetters* ☎ 0171-437 8212

Nov. London Film Festival *National Film Theatre* ☎ 0171-928 3232

INDEX BY AREA

England is famous for its pubs. Many countries try to imitate the quaint timber-framed taverns, but the only place you will find authentic olde worlde drinking establishments is on mainland Britain. London has the most diverse selection from a courtyard inn with Shakespearean galleries, dating from the 16th century, to spectacular new theme pubs.

After dark

Lamb & Flag (1)
33 Rose Street, WC2 ☎ 0171-497 9504

⊖ *Covent Garden, Leicester Square* 🕐 **Pub** *Mon.–Thur. 11am–11pm, Fri.–Sat. 11am–10.45pm, Sun. noon–10.30pm* 🍴 *Mon.-Sat. 11am–4pm* ⬛ 🎵 *Sun. 7.30pm*

The oldest pub in Covent Garden, dating from around 1627, is situated up a crooked alley. Five different cask-conditioned beers, plus a typical selection of lager, stouts, cider, wine and spirits are served. A Dixieland jazz group plays upstairs in the Dryden Room every Sunday evening.

The George Inn (2)
77 Borough High Street, SE1 ☎ 0171-407 2056 ➠ 0171-403 6613

⊖ *London Bridge, Borough* 🕐 **Pub** *Mon.–Sat. 11am–11pm, Sun. noon–10.30pm* 🍴 *daily noon–2.30pm* ⬛

An old-fashioned inn, now owned and preserved by the National Trust, still functions as a working pub and restaurant. It was rebuilt in 1667, but can be traced back to at least 1540. There is no evidence to prove that Shakespeare played here, but it is likely as he worked south of the river. The pub serves its own beer, Restoration Bitter, and also serves food.

The Orange Brewery (3)
37–39 Pimlico Road, SW1 ☎ 0171-730 5984

⊖ *Sloane Square* 🕐 **Pub** *Mon.–Sat. 11am–11pm, Sun. noon–10.30pm* 🍴 *daily noon–2.30pm* ⬛ 🍺 *Try the brasserie in the basement* ● *£3*

This 18th-century pub is renowned for having its own brewery on site and retains its traditional appearance, evoking its former days as a coffee house. Try their homemade brews such as Pimlico Porter, a rich roasted 18th-century drink, or typical English pub food such as pies flavored with beer, a huge 24oz sausage, the Cumberland Curl, or fish and chips.

King's Head (4)
115 Upper Street, N1 ☎ 0171-226 1916 ➠ 0171-226 8507

⊖ *Angel, Highbury, Islington* 🕐 **Pub** *daily. noon–midnight* **Theater** *Mon. varies; Tue.–Fri. 8pm; Sat. 3.30pm, 8pm; Sun. 3.30pm* ● *£7–11* 🍴 *Tue.–Sat. 7pm* ⬛

One of the best off-West-End theaters located in a pub, the King's Head Theatre began in 1960. The theater is located in the back of the pub and is known for its experimental plays, revivals and musicals. Pre-theater dining is available. The pub itself is typically Victorian and serves a full range of traditional British beers and spirits.

Not forgetting

⬛ **Waxy O' Connors (5)** 14–16 Rupert Street, W1 ☎ 0171-287 0255 *An Irish pub with a beech tree intertwining two stories. Specialty: fresh grilled seafood.* ⬛ **Man in the Moon (6)** 392 King's Road, SW3 ☎ 0171-351 2876 *Fringe-theater pub with lots of character.* ⬛ **Fox & Anchor (7)** 115 Charterhouse Street, Smithfield, EC1 ☎ 0171-253 4838 *Famous for its breakfasts and lunchtime steaks. Much frequented by city types and tourists.*

Pubs are often the best place to get a wholesome, good value meal at lunchtime.

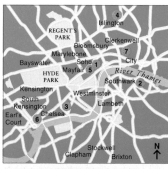

London, home to successful West-End shows and various musicals
➡ 90, is also going through a renaissance in cabaret and there are
now a number of new venues offering dining with performances by
internationally famous entertainers or fabulous floorshows. Also highly
successful are the many comedy clubs opening in town, which do not

After dark

The Comedy Store (8)
Haymarket House, I Oxendon Street, SWI
☎ **0171-344 4444 / (01426) 914433** ➡ **0171-839 7037**

🔵 *Piccadilly Circus* 🔳 **Shows** *Mon.–Thur., Sun. 8pm; Fri.–Sat. 8pm, midnight*
● *£9–£10* 🍴 🍸 *Happy Hour daily 6.30–7.30pm* ▭

London's main comedy venue where you can enjoy a bill of stand-up
comedy while you drink and eat in a fun and inexpensive environment.
Many famous names have begun here including Ben Elton, Dawn French,
Jennifer Saunders, Julian Clary and Alexei Sayle. The quality of the acts is
high and the line-up is always topical and extremely funny. Watch out for
the MC who often picks on tourists as victims of his wit (avoid the front
three rows!). Wednesday and Sunday nights are particularly good, when
the Comedy Store Players, including Josie Lawrence, Paul Merton and
Neil Mullarkey, bring you their best in comedy improvisation.

Café de Paris (9)
3–4 Coventry Street, WI ☎ **0171-734 7700** ➡ **0171-287 4861**

🔵 *Piccadilly Circus* 💃 🔳 **Dinner with floorshow** *Mon.–Fri. 7pm–4am; Sat.
8pm–4am; Sun. 7.30pm–midnight* ● *£40* **Tea dances** *Sun. 3–6.30pm* ● *£15* ▭

The world famous Café de Paris, once the ultimate in chic in the inter-
war years, was relaunched in the autumn of 1996. Fred and Adele
Astaire, Noël Coward, Marlene Dietrich, Eartha Kitt and Frank Sinatra
are just a few of the names associated with the Café's illustrious past.
As in the 1930s and 1940s, the balcony restaurant overlooks the dance
floor where a live, eight-piece band, The House of Indigo, performs
regularly during the week. Other highlights at the Café de Paris are the
Sunday afternoon tea dance with a floorshow by the London Theatre of
Ballroom featuring tango, Latin, ballet, jazz and exhibition dancing and the
'salsa fever' nights with live band held on the last Sunday of each month.
Throughout the week, diners can enjoy an international menu of classic
and contemporary cuisine – a truly hedonistic experience.

Rheingold Club (10)
Sedley Place, 361 Oxford Street, WI ☎ **0171-629 5343**

🔵 *Bond Street* 🔳 **Salsa classes** *Mon. 7–9pm* ● *£ 5* **Salsa club** *Mon. 9pm–
3am* ● *£2* **Dinner & cabaret** *Fri.–Sat. 8–9.30pm* ● *£25 (£12.50 cabaret only)*
Live band *Fri.–Sat. 9.30pm–3am* ● *£7 (Tue.–Thur., Sun. call for information)* ▭

Established in 1959, this basement club is the second oldest in London
after Ronnie Scott's ➡ 92, and has recently been renovated and made
into a late night spot for sophisticated, mature people featuring the best
international cabaret artistes, and a delicious menu created by their new
French chef Pascal Licakis. After the cabaret, the band plays until dawn.
On Monday night there is a salsa club with classes from 7–9pm.

Not forgetting
■ **Las Estrellas (11)** 2–3 Inverness Mews, W2 ☎ 0171-221 5038 / 0171-
221 8170 *Latin American dance club with classes 7–9pm and great Argentine
tango, salsa, lambada and flamenco floorshows. Bar also serves hot tapas dishes.*

offer haute cuisine, but certainly sell drinks (and bar food) which can be consumed during the show.

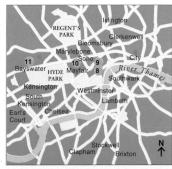

8

9

11

The West End, situated between Shaftesbury Avenue and the Strand, is celebrated for its theaterland, which is the largest in the world. Theater buffs in search of high-quality Shakespearean productions should head to the Barbican Centre and the new Globe Theatre. Other good and often innovative drama can be seen at the Royal National Theatre, the

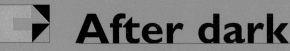

After dark

12

19

13

Royal Shakespeare Company (12)
Barbican Centre, Silk Street, EC2 ☎ 0171-638 8891

🔵 *Moorgate, Barbican* 🕐 *Nov.–Apr. (performances start around 7pm)* ● *The Pit £6–£17; The Barbican Theatre £6–£24.50* 🔲 🍴 🍸 ⊞

It is the memorable performances – from Dame Peggy Ashcroft's Queen Margaret to Barry Lynch's Puck – as well as the work of talented directors and designers that have forged the company's worldwide reputation. Productions begin in Stratford-upon-Avon and are brought to The Barbican Theatre and The Pit for six months. At certain times of the year, the Barbican Centre features a variety of international and regional theater and dance companies.

Royal National Theatre (13)
South Bank, SE1 ☎ 0171-633 0880 / reservations 0171-928 2252

🔵 *Waterloo* 🕐 *Mon.–Sat. 10am–11pm* ● *Cottesloe £16; Olivier, Lyttelton £8–£24* 🔲 🍴 *Mezzanine, Terrace Café* 🍸 *Olivier Buffet, Sandwich Bar* 🌿

London's leading repertory theater has an exciting program of classical revivals and new works. The complex has three auditoriums – the open-stage Olivier, the proscenium stage Lyttelton and the small, adaptable Cottesloe – providing a stage to suit every type of work from epics to large-scale musicals to intimate domestic dramas. The RNT also stages adaptations of foreign plays in translation.

NT
ROYAL
NATIONAL
THEATRE
PATRON H.M. THE QUEEN

Donmar Warehouse and the
Royal Court Theatre.

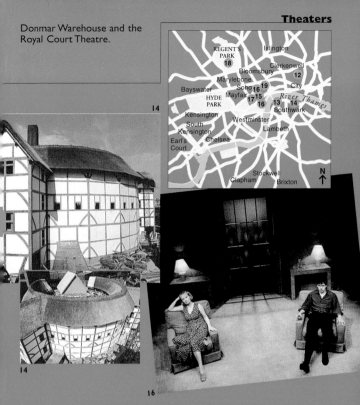

14

14

16

Shakespeare's Globe Theatre (14)
New Globe Walk, Bankside, SE1 ☎ 0171-928 6406 /
☎ 0171-620 0202 ➠ 0171-401 8261

🚇 London Bridge, Blackfriars 🕐 *Theater season* June–Sep.: Tue.–Sat. 2pm,
7.30pm; Sun. 4pm ● *gallery £20; yard £5* ◫ *Museum* ➠ *108* 📷 🎫

A replica of Shakespeare's original 'wooden O' theater, the new Globe
is a working open-air theater (May to September) with an authentic
Elizabethan experience of theatergoing. Audiences can walk around
during the performance and even interact with the actors, who have to
cope without stagelights, microphones and other modern innovations.
A second stage, The Inigo Jones Theatre, is due for completion in 1999.

Not forgetting

■ **Unicorn Arts Theatre (15)** 6–7 Great Newport Street, WC2
☎ 0171-836 3334 *High quality children's theater.* ■ **The Royal Court
Theatre (16) Downstairs** (Duke of York) St Martin's Lane, WC2 **Upstairs**
(The Ambassadors) West Street, WC2 ☎ 0171-565 5000 *Now in its
temporary home during refurbishment of its Sloane Square
base, the Royal Court presents new work as well as European
plays and forgotten classics.* ■ **Jermyn Street Theatre
(17)** 16b Jermyn Street, SW1 ☎ 0171-287 2875 *Tiny
basement theater in the heart of St James's presents cabaret,
comedy, drama and more.* ■ **Regent's Park Open Air
Theatre (18)** Regent's Park, NW1 ☎ 0171-935 5756 / ☎ 0171-486 2431
*Open-air theater in park setting with annual summer program of three plays
(two Shakespeare productions and a musical).* ■ **Donmar Warehouse
(19)** 41 Earlham Street, WC2 ☎ 0171-369 1732
*Situated in a renovated warehouse, this theater has a
small, intimate stage, and offers a varied program.*

ROYAL COURT THEATRE

Barbican Centre

Basic facts

London has a strong claim to offer the best concerts and theaters in the world. Look in the weekend broadsheets, *The Evening Standard* or *Time Out* for concert programme details as well as which plays are being staged at London's many theaters. The Royal Opera House in Floral

After dark

South Bank Centre (20)
Belvedere Road, SE1 ☎ 0171-960 4242 ➠ 0171-401 8834

🔵 Waterloo, Embankment 🕐 times vary ● prices vary 🔲 🏧 ▣ ▦

With 27 acres of land dedicated to the arts, The South Bank Centre is one of the world's largest art complexes. It consists of the Queen Elizabeth Hall, Royal Festival Hall, Purcell Room and Hayward Gallery, as well as cafés, stores, restaurants and exhibition spaces. Annual festivals include *Dance Umbrella*, *Blitz*, *Towards the Millennium*, *A Living Composer* and the multimedia extravaganza *Meltdown*. The Hayward Gallery is an art venue specializing in exhibitions of contemporary work.

Royal Albert Hall (21)
Kensington Gore, SW7 ☎ 0171-589 8212

🔵 South Kensington, Knightsbridge 🕐 *Proms* July–Sep. ● prices vary 🔲 🏧 ▣

This cavernous Victorian concert hall with its round exterior attracts performers of great stature, and it is ideal for large crowds. José Carreras, Joaquin Cortés and Eric Clapton are just some of the artists that have filled the hall. This venue can also cope with technically demanding acts such as Cirque du Soleil's *Saltimbanco*, a mix of dance, acrobatics, and opera, and The Russian All Stars' ice shows. The Royal Albert Hall is famous for its Henry Wood Promenade Concerts (known as 'The Proms'), which have taken place every year from July to September since 1894.

English National Opera at the Coliseum (22)
St Martin's Lane, WC2 ☎ 0171-632 8300 ➠ 0171-379 1264

🔵 Leicester Square, Charing Cross 🕐 Mon.–Sat. 10am–8pm *Opera* Sep.–June *Ballet* Jul.–Aug. ● £6.50–£55 🔲 ▣

Home to the English National Opera since 1968 and more recently to the English National Ballet, the Coliseum is an Edwardian music hall that has been made into a large-scale opera and ballet venue. Its tower, with a revolving globe, has become a landmark of the West End. The Coliseum makes opera as accessible as possible with great classics sung in English. It is available to visiting companies (such as the Rambert Dance Company and the Kirov Ballet) for a few weeks a year.

Not forgetting

■ **Sadler's Wells at the Peacock Theatre (23)** Portugal Street / Kingsway, WC2 ☎ 0171-314 9002 *African dance, flamenco, tango, classical ballet and contemporary dance.* ■ **Place Theatre (24)** 17 Dukes Road, WC1 ☎ 0171-387 0031 *The UK's national contemporary dance center and school.* ■ **Barbican Hall (25)** Barbican Centre, Silk Street, EC2 ☎ 0171-638 8891 *A large and comfortable modern concert venue where the London Symphony Orchestra is resident.* ■ **Wigmore Hall (26)** 36 Wigmore Street, W1 ☎ 0171-935 2141 *A concert hall built by the Bechstein piano firm, with superb chamber music programmes.* ■ **St John's Smith Square (27)** Smith Square, SW1 ☎ 0171-222 1061 *Regular lunchtime concerts. Venue in a renovated church. Good restaurant in the crypt: The Footstool.*

Street, Covent Garden, is
closed for refurbishment until
the end of 1999.

REGENT'S
PARK
Islington
24 Clerkenwell
Bloomsbury
26 23 25
Bayswater Soho City
Mayfair 22 River Thames
HYDE
PARK
20 Southwark
21 Westminster
South 27 Lambeth
Kensington
Earl's Chelsea
Court
Stockwell
Clapham Brixton
N

23

SADLER'S WELLS

21

21

St. John's, Smith Square

22

24

Basic facts

With so many blockbuster musicals from composers such as Andrew Lloyd Webber and the creative team of Boublil and Schönberg, the West End has a wide choice of shows. Many – such as *Phantom of the Opera* and *Les Misérables* – have been running for over a decade. Revivals of old

After dark

Oliver (28)
The London Palladium, 8 Argyll Street, W1 ☎ 0171-494 5020

🔵 Oxford Circus 🕐 *Theater* Mon.–Sat. 10am–8pm **Shows** Mon.–Tue., Thur., Fri. 7.30–9.30pm; Wed., Sat. 2.30–4.30pm, 7.30–9.30pm ● £10–£32.50 ▣ ▣

A major revival of Dickens's classic tale of an orphan boy who is born into a life of poverty, but is destined for higher things. Sam Mendes' sensitive staging goes some way to evoking the poverty that inspired the great 19th-century writer, but it is Lionel Bart's cheerful, catchy tunes – 'Food Glorious Food', 'Consider Yourself', 'Oom-Pah-Pah' – that steal the show.

Les Misérables (29)
The Palace Theatre, Shaftesbury Avenue, W1 ☎ 0171-434 0909

🔵 Leicester Square 🕐 *Theater* Mon.–Sat. 10am–6pm **Shows** Mon.–Wed., Fri. 7.30–10.45pm; Thur., Sat. 2.30–5.45pm, 7.30–10.45pm ● £7–£32.50 ▣ ▣

Les Misérables is more of a folk opera than a musical, with deprivation of those in need as its central theme. Based on Victor Hugo's story of ex-prisoner Jean Valjean, the play conveys the terrible living conditions of the poor in early 19th-century France, yet also shows the courage and spirit needed to survive. The musical score by Boublil and Schönberg has won over more than a generation of audiences.

Buddy (30)
The Strand Theatre, Aldwych, WC2 ☎ 0171-930 8800

🔵 Charing Cross 🕐 *Theater* Mon.–Sat. 10am–8pm **Shows** Mon.–Thur. 8–10.40pm; Fri.–Sat. 5.30–8.10pm, 8.30–11.10pm ● £4.50–£28.50 ▣ ▣

One of the first in the current wave of musicals based on the lives of legendary artists, *Buddy* celebrates the life of this recording star who died in a plane crash at the age of 21. The story traces Holly's career from his early flirtation with country music to his success as a rock 'n' roll singer-songwriter along with his band The Crickets. The last scene sees him touring as a solo artist, alongside Ritchie Valens and The Big Bopper, just before the fatal airplane trip.

Phantom of the Opera (31)
Her Majesty's Theatre, Haymarket, SW1 ☎ 0171-494 5400

🔵 Piccadilly Circus 🕐 *Theater* Mon.–Sat. 10am–6pm **Shows** Mon.–Tue, Thur., Fri. 7.45–10.15pm; Wed., Sat. 3–5.30pm, 7.45–10.15pm ● £10–£32.50 ▣ ▣

Set in 1881 at the Paris Opera House, this is Andrew Lloyd Webber's adaptation of a novel by Gaston Leroux and has some of the best costumes and special effects. It features songs such as 'All I Ask Of You', 'Masquerade' and 'Angel of Music' as well as a strong story line. The conflict between Christine, a young opera singer, her muse the Phantom and her lover Raoul is not just another love triangle, but musical at its best.

Not forgetting

■ **Player's Theatre (32)** The Arches, Villiers Street, WC2 ☎ 0171-839 1134 *Traditional Victorian music hall with a restaurant serving English food.*

classics, such as *Oliver!*, appear from time to time and there's still a trend for tributes to pop, rock and jazz legends – *Buddy* has run for eight years.

28

28

29

28

31

30

31

Basic facts

One of the oldest jazz clubs in the world, the celebrated Ronnie Scott's, is situated in London. The number of jazz clubs continues to grow and diversify. Music is at the heart of the entertainment at any jazz venue worth its salt, but nowadays you are not just there to listen. Modern jazz

After dark

Ronnie Scott's (33)
47 Frith Street, Soho, W1 ☎ 0171-439 0747 ➡ 0171-437 5081

🔵 *Leicester Square* 🕐 *Mon.–Sat. 8.30pm–3am* ● *£15 ('Upstairs at Ronnie's' disco only): Wed., Thur. £6; Fri., Sat. £8)* 🔳 🍴 🍸 🎵

London's premier jazz club has featured legendary names for almost 40 years – including Ella Fitzgerald, Dizzy Gillespie, Roy Ayers, Irakere, Hugh Masekela, Bob Berg, Michel Petrucciani and Charlie Watts. Artists, often from the US, appear for up to three weeks supported by a British group. Ronnie Scott himself died in 1996. The interior is cozy with subdued lighting and photos of musicians on the walls. The inexpensive menu is available all evening. 'Upstairs at Ronnie's' has Club Latino on Friday and Saturday with salsa dancing and a 1970s disco on Wednesday and Thursday.

100 Club (34)
100 Oxford Street, W1 ☎ 0171-636 0933 ➡ 0171-436 1958

🔵 *Tottenham Court Road, Oxford Circus* 🕐 *Mon.–Wed. 7.30pm–midnight; Thur. 8pm–midnight; Fri. 8.30pm–3am; Sat. 7.30pm–1am; Sun. 7.30–11pm* ● *£5–£8 (Jazz: Fri. noon–3pm● free)* 🔳 🍸 🎵

This friendly basement venue might be a little shabby, but it still attracts lots of high-profile performers. With a small dance floor, the club places an emphasis on dance bands including jump, jive and swing from groups like Too Darn Hot, 1920s music from the Charleston Chasers and boogie woogie from Campbell Burnap, as well as New Orleans or classic jazz. The bar serves drinks at near pub prices and there's a snack bar.

606 Club (35)
90 Lots Road, SW10 ☎ 0171-352 5953 ➡ 0171-349 0655

🔵 *Fulham Broadway, Earl's Court* 🕐 *Mon.–Sat. 8.30pm–2am; Sun. 8.30–11.30pm* ● *£4.25–£4.95* 🔳 🍴 🎵

The 606 Club near Chelsea Harbour is a private members' jazz cellar, hidden behind a red brick arched doorway with a wait-for-an-answer doorbell. There are gigs every night and non-members are welcome, so long as you eat. Unlike some jazz clubs, the food here is delicious ranging from staples such as shepherd's pie and hamburgers to baked salmon fillet stuffed with oyster mushrooms or roast rack of lamb, all cooked with the freshest ingredients. The music covers the entire jazz spectrum with an emphasis on modern jazz trios and quartets, many of whom are established names and others who are up and coming. Musicians come here to jam after their other gigs – surely a good recommendation.

Not forgetting

■ **Pizza on the Park (36)** 11 Knightsbridge, SW1 ☎ 0171-235 5273 *Excellent jazz club in a good pizzeria.* ■ **Jazz Café (37)** 5 Parkway, Camden Town, NW1 ☎ 0171-344 0044 *Voted best club 1995 by Blues and Soul Magazine.* ■ **Pizza Express Jazz Club (38)** 10 Dean Street, Soho, W1 ☎ 0171-439 8722 (jazz club) / ☎ 0171-437 9595 (restaurant) *Jazz venue and pizzeria.* ■ **Dover Street Wine Bar (39)** 8–9 Dover Street, W1 ☎ 0171-629 9813 *Wine bar. Jazz, blues, soul and swing.*

clubs mix cool music with gourmet food, fine wine, dancing and beer. The Soho Jazz Festival is held in September and October.

35

37

Soho is still at the heart of the London jazz scene and each year the Soho Jazz Festival is held in September and October ➡ 81.

36

33

36

Basic facts

Whatever music you're into – deep and funky house and techno, or Latin rhythms like salsa, soca or merengue, or hard-edged garage – London has one of the widest range of clubs. Venues may offer the ultimate in glamor or be spartan black spaces where the essential

After dark

Ministry of Sound (40)
103 Gaunt Street, SE1 ☎ 0171-378 6528 ➡ 0171-403 5348

🚇 *Elephant & Castle* 🕐 *Fri. 10.30pm–6.30am; Sat. midnight–9am* ● *Fri. £10; Sat. £15* 🔲 🍸

What began as an underground nightclub in 1991 is now spoken about as the best nightclub ever. No one who has entered the Main Room (or the Box), which is all dance floor, can fully describe the physical effect of this legendary sound system. A line-up of DJs play techno, house and garage. Soundproofed tunnels lead to the Bar, with its fantastic sound system, and into the Playstation (full of gaming machines), The Atmosbar, the Cinema Bar (showing Laserdisc movies) and upstairs, to the Space Bar, where you can hear drum 'n' bass, jungle, hip hop and jazz.

Velvet Underground (41)
143 Charing Cross Road, WC2
☎ 0171-439 4655 ➡ 0171-734 0819

🚇 *Tottenham Court Road* 🕐 *Mon., Thur. 10pm–3am; Tue. varies; Wed. 10.30pm–3am; Fri.–Sat. 10.30pm–4am* ● *Mon. £5; Tue.–Thur. prices vary; Fri.–Sat. £10* 🔲 🍸

A young mixed crowd frequents this small, stylish club with velvet-covered walls and ceiling where you can hear a mix of the best garage, 'handbag' house and club classics from DJs such as World Recession, Ultimate Base, Ego Trip and The Tomorrow People. The dance floor is tiny, but has several different levels. The decoration consists of pink and purple hearts, framed Barbie Dolls, mirror mosaics and Seventies-style tubes of bubbling water that light up a cozy area with sofas and divans.

Heaven (42)
Under the Arches, Villiers Street, WC2
☎ 0171-930 2020 ➡ 0171-930 8306

🚇 *Embankment, Charing Cross* 🕐 *Tue.–Sat. 10.30pm–3.30am, Sun. 9.30pm–2am (gay night)* ● *£3; £6 after 11pm; £7 after midnight* 🔲 🍸

The best gay club in London, Heaven is a cavernous venue situated under the railway arches, with three separate dance floors. The main hall has an overhead gallery and resting areas under the arches with huge prison bars. The two other dance areas are large: one has a wrought-iron tree growing around the room, the other has colored balloons. Respected for its music, this venue attracts some of London's trendiest clubbers. Hibernation plays techno on Thursday, garage on Fridays and Fruit Machine and Made In Heaven take over on Wednesday and Saturday.

Not forgetting

■ **Stringfellows (43)** 16–19 Upper St Martin's Lane, WC2 ☎ 0171-240 5534 *Restaurant and piano bar at street level. Bars and dance floor in the basement. Topless table-dancers during the week.* ■ **Bar Rumba (44)** 36 Shaftesbury Avenue, W1 ☎ 0171-287 2715 *Basement bar and nightclub. Salsa classes and club on Tuesday.* ■ **Hippodrome (45)** Hippodrome Corner, Leicester Square, WC2 ☎ 0171-437 4311 *This enormous ever-popular discotheque is a favorite with tourists.*

feature is the sound system. There are often long queues to get into nightclubs on Friday and Saturday nights.

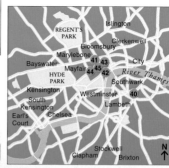

41

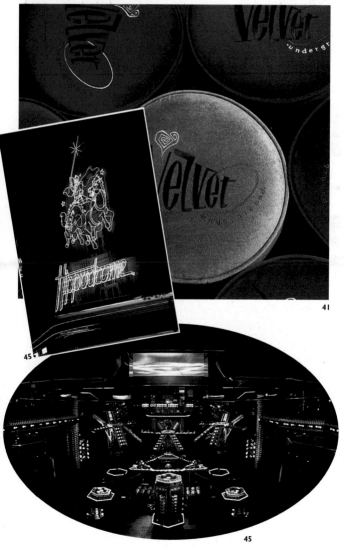

41

45

45

White card

This card gives free entry to 15 London museums and galleries. Available from tourist offices and participating museums and galleries. Price: £15 (3 days); £25 (7 days).

Bus routes 11 and 15

Jump on a number 11 bus (running from Victoria to Liverpool Street) or a number (Marble Arch to the Tower of London) to see London's major monuments for the price of a single bus ticket ➤ 13.

Bus tours
Guided tours
(2 hours) in an
open-top bus
(£10).
☎ 0181-877 1722

River trips
Embark at
Tower Bridge or
Westminster.
City Cruise
☎ 0171-515 1415

Canal trips
Sail along Regent's Canal
from Little Venice or Camden Lock.
Jason's Trip ☎ 0171-286 3428
Jenny Wren ☎ 0171-485 4433
London Waterbus ☎ 0171-482 2550

71

Sights

THE INSIDER'S FAVORITES

On foot
Thematic tours.
Original Walks
☎ 0171-624 3978
Historical Tours
☎ 0181-668 4019

Tailor-made
Specially
designed tours
from £130 per
day. *Tour Guides*
☎ 0171-495 5504

By helicopter
30-minute flights along the Thames,
departing from Biggin Hill Airport,
12 miles southwest of London. ● £99
Biggin Hill Airport ☎ (01959) 540803

INDEX BY TYPE

In the area

This stretch of the Thames was once the busiest port in Europe. Nowadays the old docks and warehouses are being rebuilt as offices, stores, restaurants, tourist attractions and residential flats. ■ Where to eat ➡ 78 ■ After dark ➡ 82

What to see

Tower of London (1)
Tower Hill, EC3 ☎ 0171-709 0765

⊖ Tower Hill ⏰ Mar.–Oct.: Mon.–Sat. 9am–5pm, Sun. 10am–5pm; Nov. 1–Apr.: Sun.–Mon. 10am–4pm, Tue.–Sat. 9am–4pm ● £8.50; seniors, students £6.40; children £5.60 ⛔

For over 900 years the Tower, overlooking the river and the City from the east, has served as a formidable fortress, palace and prison. Allow at least two hours for a tour with the Yeoman Warders, in their Tudor uniform, to see the Norman 'White Tower' and chapel, the medieval palace and dungeons, the resident ravens, and the impressive Crown Jewels. If your time is limited, there are views over the Tower from Tower Hill (near the subway) or from Tower Bridge.

Tower Bridge (2)
Visitors entrance to the far north of the bridge
☎ 0171-378 1928 / Bridge Lift Information ☎ 0171-378 7700

⊖ Tower Hill ⏰ Apr.–Oct.: daily 10am–6.30pm Nov.–Mar.: daily 9.30am–5.45pm ● £5.50; students, children £3.75 ⊞ ⛔

Since its grand opening on June 30, 1894, Tower Bridge has become one of London's most distinctive landmarks. The original steam engines (in use until 1976) can still be seen, and there are great views from the upper walkway. Telephone the bridge lift information line to find out when the bridge will be raised for ships to pass through.

Design Museum (3)
28 Shad Thames, SE1 ☎ 0171-378 6055

⊖ Tower Hill, London Bridge ⏰ Mon.–Fri. 11.30am–6pm; Sat., Sun. noon–6pm ● £4.75; students, children £3.50; White Card ⊞ 🖥 ⛔

Sir Terence Conran, whose Conran Shop ➡ 154 and stylish restaurants have set new trends in design, was the force behind this innovative museum, in a converted warehouse. Exhibits range from well-known classics in furniture, cars and household goods to the latest in contemporary design. The Blueprint Cafe ➡ 78 has a balcony overlooking the river.

Not forgetting

■ **St Katharine's Dock (4)** Open 24 hours daily. Old docks transformed into a marina with stores, restaurants and the Dickens Inn.
■ **Monument (5)** Monument Street, EC2 ☎ 0171-626 2717 ⏰ Apr.–Sep.: Mon.–Fri. 9am–5.40pm; Sat.–Sun. 2–5.40pm / Oct.–Mar.: Mon.–Sat. 9am–3.40pm Built by Christopher Wren, 202-ft high column, with viewing platform, commemorating the Great Fire of London in 1666.
■ **HMS Belfast (6)** Tooley Street, SE1 ☎ 0171-407 6434 ⏰ Mar.–Oct.: daily 10am–6pm / Nov.–Feb.: daily. 10am–5pm 11½-ton World War II cruise ship.
■ **London Dungeon (7)** 28–34 Tooley Street, SE1 ☎ 0171-403 7221 ⏰ Apr.–Sep.: daily 10am–5.30pm / Oct.–Mar.: daily 10am–4.30pm Dark, dank vaults displaying gruesome waxworks of medieval torture, plague, murder and executions.
■ **The Old Operating Theatre (8)** 9a St Thomas Street, SE1 ☎ 0171-955 4791 ⏰ daily 10am–4pm 9th-century operating theater.

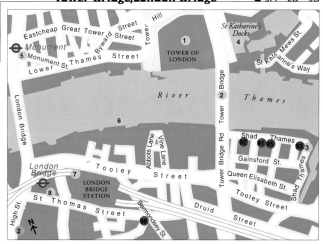

Surgeons once performed amputations in this sawdust-covered room, situated just above the church.

In the area

The old city was founded by the Romans in AD 43–50. The medieval street plan and parts of the Roman Wall survive. The City is now mainly a center for business and finance, deserted in the evenings and at weekends. ■ Where to eat ➡ 70 ■ After dark ➡ 82 ➡ 86 ➡ 88

What to see

St Paul's Cathedral (9)
Chapter House, St Paul's Church Yard, EC4 ☎ 0171-236 4128

🚇 St Paul's 🕐 daily 8.30am–4pm ● **Cathedral and crypt** £3.50; children £2.50 **Cathedral, crypt and galleries** £6; children £3 ♿

This cathedral replaced the huge Gothic church which burned down in the Great Fire of 1666. Designed by Christopher Wren, the dome (360ft high) dominated the city's skyline when it was completed in 1710; there are breathtaking views from the galleries. In the crypt are the tombs of Nelson and Wellington, and Wren's Great Model for the cathedral.

Guildhall (10)
Guildhall Yard, Gresham Street, EC2 ☎ 0171-606 3030

🚇 Bank, St Paul's 🕐 May–Sep.: daily 10am–5pm Oct. 1–Apr.: Mon.–Sat. 10am–5pm **Clock Museum** Mon.–Fri. 9.30am–4.30pm ● free

Guildhall has been the center of local city government for over 700 years. The 15th-century Great Hall (open to visitors) still holds ceremonial events. The adjoining post-war buildings house the Guildhall Library and a unique Clock Museum with over 700 clocks and watches.

Museum of London (11)
London Wall (High Walk), EC2 ☎ 0171-600 3699

🚇 Barbican, St Paul's 🕐 Tue.–Sat. 10am–5.50pm; Sun. noon–5.50pm ● £4; students and under-17s £2; under-5s entrance free; White Card

Built in 1976 as part of the Barbican redevelopment, this museum tells the story of London and its people from prehistory to the present. See the displays on Roman London (AD 43–410), the model of old London Bridge (demolished in 1831), the Great Fire exhibit, and the Lord Mayor's Coach (still used each November for the Lord Mayor's Show).

St Bartholomew the Great (12)
West Smithfield, EC1 ☎ 0171-606 5171

🚇 Barbican, Farringdon, St Paul's 🕐 Mon.–Fri. 8.30am–5pm (4pm in winter); Sat. 10.30am–1.30pm; Sun. 8–10am ● free

This is the oldest parish church in the City, founded in 1123, and was once part of the ancient priory and hospital of St Bartholomew. Its arches and pillars are an impressive example of Norman (Romanesque) architecture. Nearby is historic Smithfield, once the scene of public executions, now the site of one of Europe's largest meat markets.

Not forgetting

■ **Bank of England Museum (13)** Bartholomew Lane, EC2 ☎ 0171-601 5545 🕐 Mon.–Fri. 10am–5pm *Charts the history of the bank of England.* ■ **Lloyd's (14)** 1 Lime Street, EC3 *Spectacular piece of modern architecture designed by Richard Rogers (no visits).* ■ **Leadenhall Market (15)** Whittington Avenue, EC3 🕐 Mon.–Fri. 7am–3pm *Victorian-style covered market.* ■ **St Mary-le-Bow (16)** Cheapside, EC2 ☎ 0171-248 5139 🕐 Mon.–Thur. 6.30am–6pm; Fri. 6.30am–4.15pm *Elegant church by Wren.*

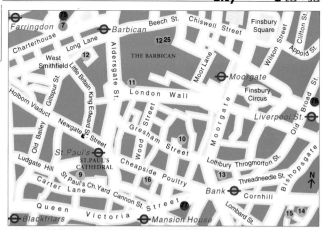

The City of London has its own mayor and its own governing body, separate from Westminster.

What to see

British Museum (17)
Great Russell Street, WC1 ☎ 0171-636 1555 / 0171-580 1788

⊖ Tottenham Court Road, Holborn ◷ Mon.–Sat. 10am–5pm; Sun. 2.30–6pm ● free 🎫 *Museum* Mon.–Sat. 11.15am, 2.15pm; Sun. 3pm, 3.30pm ● £6 *British Library* Mon.–Fri. 2.15–4.15pm ● free

Founded in 1753, the British Museum contains a fabulous collection of classical antiquities, archeological finds, prints, drawings and coins, filling 94 galleries. Exhibits include the Rosetta Stone (room 25) which provided the key to deciphering Egyptian hieroglyphs; the Elgin Marbles (room 8) which once adorned the Parthenon, and the Egyptian mummy collection (rooms 60, 61). The magnificent domed Reading Room will be incorporated into the museum with the relocation of the British Library to its new site at Euston.

Sir John Soane's Museum (18)
13 Lincoln's Inn Fields, WC2 ☎ 0171-405 2107

⊖ Holborn ◷ Tue.–Sat. 10am–5pm; first Tue. in the month 6–9pm ● free

Sir John Soane (1753–1837), chief architect of the Bank of England, lived here for the last 24 years of his life and gathered an extraordinary collection of art and archeological finds. His paintings include works by Canaletto, Turner, Piranesi and the complete set of Hogarth's originals for *The Rake's Progress* (1734). Soane left his house and its contents to the nation, to be displayed as it was in his lifetime.

Courtauld Institute Galleries (19)
Somerset House, Strand, WC2 ☎ 0171-873 2526

⊖ Covent Garden ◷ Mon.–Sat. 10am–6pm; Sun. 2–6pm ● £4; students £3; seniors £2; under-18s free; White Card 💳

The best collection of Impressionist and Post-Impressionist paintings in London, amassed by textile magnate Samuel Courtauld, is now housed in the Georgian terraces of Somerset House (former home of the Royal Academy). Works by Cranach, Botticelli, Tiepolo and Rubens, Manet's *Bar at the Folies-Bergère* and Van Gogh's *Self Portrait with Bandaged Ear*.

Not forgetting
■ **Inns of Court** (20) *Law students and barristers have been educated here since the Middle Ages: Gray's Inn, where Charles Dickens was once a clerk; the oldest, Lincoln's Inn; Inner and Middle Temple. The most remarkable buildings are Temple Church (1179–85) and Middle Temple Hall (1700s).* ■ **Cabaret Mechanical Theatre** (21) Covent Garden Market, WC2 ☎ 0171-379 7961 ◷ Easter–Sep.: Mon.–Sat. 10am–7pm; Sun. 11am–7pm / Oct.–Easter: Mon.–Sat. 10am–6.30pm; Sun. 11am–6.30pm *Unique collection of mechanical models.* ■ **London Transport Museum** (22) Covent Garden Piazza, WC2 ☎ 0171-379 6344 ◷ Mon.–Thur., Sat., Sun. 10am–5.15pm; Fri. 11am–5.15pm *In the former flower market. History of London Transport from the first buses and trams to the latest tubes.* ■ **Theatre Museum** (23) Russell Street, WC2 ☎ 0171-836 7891 ◷ Tue.–Sun. 11am–7pm *History of theater, ballet and opera.*

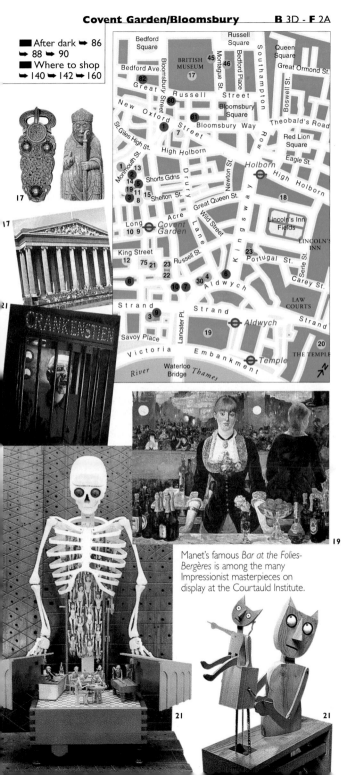

■ After dark ➡ 86
➡ 88 ➡ 90
■ Where to shop
➡ 140 ➡ 142 ➡ 160

Manet's famous *Bar at the Folies-Bergères* is among the many Impressionist masterpieces on display at the Courtauld Institute.

In the area

Piccadilly Circus is at the heart of London's West End. ■ Where to stay
➠ 20 ➠ 24 ■ Where to eat ➠ 48 ➠ 50 ➠ 52 ➠ 54 ➠ 56 ■ After
dark ➠ 82 ➠ 84 ➠ 86 ➠ 94 ■ What to see ➠ 118 ■ Where to
shop ➠ 144 ➠ 146 ➠ 148 ➠ 150 ➠ 152 ➠ 160

What to see

Piccadilly Circus (24)

⊖ *Piccadilly Circus*

The graceful fountain statue of Eros, standing in Piccadilly Circus since
1893, has become a symbol of touristy London and a well-known
meeting point. Its official title, *The Angel of Christian Charity*, was intended
to commemorate Victorian philanthropist, the Earl of Shaftesbury, who
campaigned against child labor, and gave his name to Shaftesbury Avenue.

Royal Academy of Arts (25)
Burlington House, Piccadilly W1 ☎ 0171-439 7438

⊖ *Green Park, Piccadilly* 🕓 *daily 10am–6pm* ● *£4.50–£6; seniors, students
£3.50–£4; under-11s £1–£1.25; White Card* 🔲 🍴

The Royal Academy was founded in 1768 to teach and exhibit the fine
arts. Its home is the early 18th-century Palladian mansion built for Lord
Burlington, where it houses exhibitions throughout the year in three
splendid galleries. The famous Summer Exhibition (June to August)
displays thousands of contemporary paintings, drawings, sculptures and
architectural works that are all for sale.

Museum of Mankind (26)
6 Burlington Gardens, W1 ☎ 0171-437 2224 / 0171-323 8043

⊖ *Green Park, Piccadilly* 🕓 *Mon.–Sat. 10am–5pm; Sun. 2.30–6pm* ● *free* 🔳 🔲
The Columbia

The ethnography department of the British Museum occupies this
uncrowded, spacious building, with fine displays of ethnic arts and crafts,
costumes, masks, weapons and musical instruments. The superb special
exhibitions are always worth a visit, and they also have free movies,
a good store and excellent café.

Trocadero (27)
1 Piccadilly Circus, W1 ☎ 0171-439 1791 ➠ 0171-434 1413

⊖ *Piccadilly Circus* 🕓 *daily 10am–noon* ● *Segaworld £2 (plus the cost of rides)*

The former music hall has been transformed into an enormous shopping
and entertainment complex on four stories. Segaworld, based on the
Joypolis Park in Japan, is the big attraction here, with six 'virtual reality'
rides (adult £12, child £9). You will also find Europe's largest video wall,
a seven-screen MGM movie theater and the only 3-D movie theater in
London.

Not forgetting

■ **Rock Circus (28)** The London Pavilion, 1 Piccadilly Circus, W1
☎ 0171-734 7203 🕓 Mon., Wed., Thur., Sun. 11am–9pm; Tue. noon–9pm; Fri.,
Sat. 11am–10pm *Wax rock stars and their music, from the Beatles to Prince and
Madonna.*
■ **St James's Church (29)** 197 Piccadilly, W1 ☎ 0171-734 4511 🕓
daily 8.30am–7pm *Christopher Wren's only West End church (1684) with a crafts
market, regular concerts and a vegetarian café.*

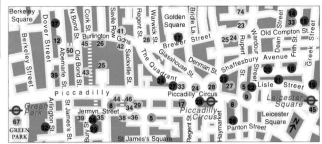

24

Piccadilly Circus
divides the elegant
districts of
St James's and
Mayfair from
bustling Covent
Garden and Soho.

25

25

25

In the area

Once the site of royal stables, the square was laid out in the 1830s to commemorate the Battle of Trafalgar (October 21, 1805), in which Admiral Lord Nelson was victorious over the French and Spanish navy. Whitehall, leading to Westminster, is home to government ministries and

What to see

The National Gallery (30)
Trafalgar Square, WC2 ☎ 0171-747 2484 / 0171-747 2885

⊖ Charing Cross 🕐 Mon.–Tue., Thur.–Sat. 10am–6pm; Wed. 10am–8pm; Sun. noon–4pm ● free 🎧 Mon.–Fri. 11am, 2.30pm; Sat. 2pm, 3.30pm; Sun. 12.30pm ● free 🏢 🛈

One of the world's greatest collections of paintings from all the leading European schools, including Italian, Dutch, Flemish, Spanish, French and British, arranged chronologically, from the early Renaissance (new Sainsbury Wing) to Impressionists and early 20th-century (room 43–46).

Trafalgar Square & Nelson's Column (31)

⊖ Charing Cross (Trafalgar Square exit)

Nelson stands atop the 171ft column, guarded by four huge, bronze lions. The base of the column is decorated with friezes showing four of Nelson's famous battles, including his death at Trafalgar aboard the HMS Victory. This is a favorite gathering point for people, pigeons and political demonstrations. Each year an enormous Christmas tree is erected here.

Horse Guards Parade (32)
Whitehall, SW1 ☎ 0171-930 4466

⊖ Charing Cross 🕐 **Horse Guards** summer: 10am–5pm / winter : 10am–4pm **Changing of the guard** Mon.–Sat. 11am; Sun. 10am **Trooping of the Colour** 2nd or 3rd Sat. in June

Horse Guards is the headquarters of the Household Division (the soldiers who guard the Queen). Two mounted sentries from the cavalry stand guard at the Whitehall entrance from 10am to 4pm daily, on their splendid black horses. Facing St James's Park, the hugh Horse Guards Parade is the scene of the *Trooping of the Colour*.

Cabinet War Rooms (33)
Clive Steps, King Charles Street, SW1 ☎ 0171-930 6961

⊖ Westminster 🕐 Apr.–Oct. 9.30–5.15pm; Nov.–Mar. 10am–5.15pm ● £4.40; seniors, students £3.30; children £2.20

The underground headquarters for Sir Winston Churchill's War Cabinet during World War II, preserved exactly at the end of the war. See Churchill's spartan bedroom and the all-important Map Room, manned night and day throughout the war. The taped guide is very worthwhile.

Not forgetting

■ **National Portrait Gallery (34)** 2 St Martin's Place, WC2 ☎ 0171-306 0055 🕐 Mon.–Sat. 10am–6pm; Sun. noon–6pm *Paintings, sculptures and photographs of the famous and infamous.* ■ **St Martin-in-the-Fields (35)** Trafalgar Square, WC2 ☎ 0171-930 1862 🕐 daily 9am–6pm *The oldest building in the square (1726), distinctive portico, tower and steeple, and free lunchtime concerts.* ■ **Banqueting House (36)** Whitehall, SW1 ☎ 0171-930 4179 🕐 Mon.–Sat. 10am–4pm *London's first renaissance building (Inigo Jones, 1622) whence Charles I stepped to the scaffold.*

the Prime Minister's residence
at 10 Downing Street.
■ After dark ➤ 90 ■ What
to see ➤ 118

In the area

The South Bank is one of the most exciting developments in the capital. The best way to see it is to follow the riverside walkway (Queen's Walk) east from Waterloo Bridge to London Bridge. ■ Where to eat ➡ 76 ■ After dark ➡ 82 ➡ 86 ➡ 88

What to see

Museum of the Moving Image (MOMI) (37)
South Bank, SE1 ☎ 0171-401 2636 / 0171-815 1350

⊖ Waterloo, Embankment 🕒 daily 10am–5pm ● £5.95; students £4.85; seniors, children £4; White Card

This entertaining museum, next to the National Film Theatre, tells the story of the movies, television and animation, from the first optical toys to the latest special effects. You can make your own cartoon strip, take a screen test (with real actors), or watch the hundreds of movie clips, from Charlie Chaplin and silent movies to newsreels, Russian classics and Hollywood favorites.

Oxo Tower (38)
Oxo Tower Wharf, Bargehouse Street, SE1 ☎ 0171-401 3610

⊖ Waterloo, Blackfriars 🕒 daily 10am–10pm 🏢 Tue.–Sun. 11am–6pm
🍸 🍴 The Oxo Tower, Restaurant & Brasserie ➡ 76, The Bistrot Riverside 🏖

The 1930s art deco tower, with its distinctive OXO logo, is the focus for a new complex of designer-studios and stores, cafés, bars and the rooftop Harvey Nichols Restaurant. Take the elevator to the viewing platform for great views over the river and north bank.

Globe Theatre & Shakespeare Museum (39)
New Globe Walk, Bankside, SE1 ☎ 0171-928 6406

⊖ London Bridge, Mansion House 🕒 Museum daily 10am–5pm ● £5; seniors, students £4; children £3 🎫 (running time 40 mins) 🏢 💺 Theater ➡ 86

The original Globe Theatre, where Shakespeare's plays were staged during his lifetime, has been reconstructed, complete with thatched roof and a circular theater designed to use natural light and a minimum of scenery. There is also a museum, an education center and a cafe.

Royal Festival Hall (40)
south of Waterloo Bridge, South Bank, SE1 ☎ 0171-960 4242

⊖ Waterloo 🕒 daily 10am–10pm 🍴 People's Palace ➡ 76 🍸 🎵 daily 12.30–2pm

This large concert hall, built for the 1951 Festival of Britain, is the main focus of the South Bank Centre ➡ 88 (also comprising Queen Elizabeth Hall, the Purcell Room and Hayward Gallery). The light, spacious building is open daily with a lively program of concerts, free exhibitions and foyer events, bars and restaurants, and an excellent bookstore. On summer weekends, there are outdoor events on the riverside terraces.

Not forgetting

■ **The Clink Prison (41)** 1 Clink Street, SE1 ☎ 0171-403 6515
🕒 daily 10am–6pm On the site of the old Clink Prison, this tiny museum charts the medieval lowlife of the area.
■ **Southwark Cathedral (42)** Montague Close, SE1 ☎ 0171-407 2939
🕒 Mon.–Fri. 8am–6pm; Sat. 9am–6pm; Sun. 8.45am–6pm The former monastic church, with 13th-century foundations and Gothic choir, became an Anglican cathedral in 1905.

Queen's Walk, or Silver Jubilee Walkway, provides a delightful riverside walk.

What to see

Buckingham Palace (43)
The Mall, SW1 ☎ 0171-930 4832

🚇 St James's Park, Green Park 🕐 Aug. and Sep.: daily. 9.30–4.15pm ● £9; seniors £6.50; children £5

The Royal Standard flies over the Palace when the Queen is in residence. The elegant State Apartments are now open to visitors for two months in the summer, while the royal family are on holiday in Scotland. The 18 rooms on view include the Throne Room, the State Dining Room, the Picture Gallery with masterpieces from the Royal Collection, and the semicircular Music Room overlooking the garden.

Changing of the Guard (44)
Buckingham Palace, SW1 ☎ (0839) 123411 / (0891) 505452

🚇 St James's Park, Green Park 🕐 Apr.–July: daily 11.27am / Aug.–Apr.: alternate days 11.27am

One of the five infantry regiments (Grenadiers, Coldstream, Scots, Irish and Welsh) stand guard at Buckingham Palace, in their scarlet jackets and bearskin hats. The ceremony begins with the gathering of the new guard in the forecourt of Wellington Barracks, in Birdcage Walk, from 10.45am. At 11.27am precisely they march across to the Palace forecourt for the half-hour ceremony. Less crowded is the Changing of the Horseguards at Whitehall at 10.30am.

Royal Mews (45)
Buckingham Palace Road, SW1 ☎ 0171-930 4832

🚇 Victoria 🕐 Apr.–July: Tue.–Thur. noon–4pm / Aug.–Sep.: Mon.–Thur. 10.30am–4.30pm / Oct.–Mar.: Wed. noon–4pm ● £3.70; seniors £2.60; children £2.10

The royal carriages and horses, still used for ceremonial occasions, are kept at the Royal Mews (once used for keeping falcons and hawks when 'mewing' or molting – hence the name). The ornate Golden Coronation Coach, the Glass Coach used for royal weddings, and many more are on view here, with rooms displaying gleaming tack. The royal limousines are on display next door.

Not forgetting

■ **Queen's Gallery (46)** Buckingham Palace Road, SW1 ☎ 0171-799 2331 🕐 daily 9.30am–4pm *Changing exhibitions of paintings and other precious objects from the Royal Collection are on display here.*
■ **Apsley House (47)** Hyde Park Corner, W1 ☎ 0171-499 5676 🕐 Tue.–Sun. 11am–4.30pm *Residence of the first Duke of Wellington (1769–1852), general and statesman, who defeated Napoleon at Waterloo.*
■ **Guards Museum (48)** Wellington Barracks, Birdcage Walk, SW1 ☎ 0171-414 3430 🕐 daily 10am–4pm *Small museum tells the 300-year history of the Foot Guards, with uniforms, weapons and background music.*
■ **Westminster Cathedral (49)** Victoria Street, SW1 ☎ 0171-798 9055 🕐 daily 7am–7pm (elevation to the bell tower Apr.–Oct.: daily 9am–5pm / Nov.–Mar.: Thur.–Sun. 9am–5pm) *Striking red-and-white Byzantine-style Roman Catholic cathedral with great views from the bell tower (273ft).*

to eat ➥ 54 ➥ 58
■ What to see ➥ 118

The Royal Mews house the carriages and horses used for ceremonial occasions.

43

43

43

45

49

43

In the area

Westminster has been the center for the royal court and government since the mid-11th century, when King Edward the Confessor built his new palace and splendid abbey church here, two miles west of the City – hence the name 'West Minster'. Since then Westminster has become

What to see

Westminster Abbey (50)
Dean's Yard, SW1 ☎ 0171-222 5152 / visits ☎ 0171-222 7110

🚇 *Westminster* 🕐 ***Nave and cloisters*** *Mon.–Sat. 8am–6pm* ● *free* ***Royal chapels*** *Mon.–Fri. 9am–3.45pm; Sat. 9am–1.45pm, 3.45-4.45pm* ● *£4 (Wed. £2); seniors, students £2; children £1* ***Chapter House and Abbey Museum*** *Mar. 16–Oct. 15: daily 10.30am–5.30pm; Oct. 16–Mar. 15: 9.30am–3.30pm* ● *£2.50; seniors, students £1.90; children £1.30* 🎫 *Mon.–Fri.* ● *£7*

Every king and queen of England since William the Conqueror (1066) has been crowned here, and many are buried here. See the Coronation Chair (1296) and the Royal Chapels beyond the 13th-century nave, now with many monuments to famous citizens, including Poets' Corner. The octagonal Chapter House (1253), in Early English Gothic style, and the fan-vaulted roof in the Henry VII Chapel, are just two of the highlights here, and the Abbey Museum in the Norman undercroft is worth a visit. Wednesday evening is usually a quieter (and cheaper) time to visit.

Houses of Parliament and Big Ben (51)
Westminster Palace, SW1 ☎ 0171-219 4272 (House of Commons) / ☎ 0171-219 3107 (House of Lords)

🚇 *Westminster* 🕐 ***Parliament*** *mid-Oct.–mid-Jul. (open when Commons and Lords are sitting)* ***House of Commons*** *Mon.–Tue., Thur. 2.30–10.30pm; Wed. 9.30am–2pm, 2.30–10.30pm; Fri. 9.30am–3pm* ***House of Lords*** *telephone to check times* ● *free*

When Henry VIII moved to Whitehall Palace in 1532, the old Palace of Westminster became the permanent seat of Parliament. Today's neo-Gothic building, complete with the clock tower Big Ben, was opened in 1852, after the old palace burned down in 1834. The medieval Westminster Hall and Jewel Tower (see below) are the only surviving parts of original palace. Anyone can watch the debates in the House of Commons and the House of Lords from the Visitors' Gallery.

Tate Gallery (52)
Millbank, SW1 ☎ 0171-887 8000

🚇 *Pimlico* 🕐 *daily 10am–5.50pm* ● *free* 🖼 *daily 10.30am–5.30pm* 🍽 *Mon.–Sat. noon–3pm*

The national collections of British and 20th-century art are exhibited here. The old Bankside Power Station is to be transformed into the new Tate Gallery of Modern Art (due to be completed in 2000). The superb Turner collection, left to the nation by the landscape artist J.M.W. Turner (1775–1851), is now displayed in the adjacent Clore Gallery, opened in 1987.

Not forgetting

■ **St Margaret's (53)** Parliament Square, SW1 ☎ 0171-222 6382 🕐 Mon.–Sat. 9.30am–5pm *15th-century parish church for the House of Commons, with some excellent stained glass.* ■ **Jewel Tower (54)** Abingdon Street, SW1 ☎ 0171-222 2219 🕐 Apr.–Sep.: daily 10am–1pm, 2–6pm / Oct.–Mar.: daily 10am–1pm, 2–4pm *14th-century moated tower now houses an exhibition on Parliament past and present.*

synonymous with British parliamentary life and politics. The palace's highest tower, Big Ben, dates back more than a century. ■ After dark ➡ 88

52

52

51

50

Big Ben chimed for the first time on May 1, 1859 and has only broken down three times.

50

51

The South Kensington museums and colleges were built from the profits of the Great Exhibition of 1851, which attracted six million people from all over the world. ■ Where to stay ➡ 32 ■ Where to eat ➡ 62 ■ After dark ➡ 88 ■ What to see ➡ 118 ■ Where to shop ➡ 154

What to see

Victoria & Albert Museum (55)
Cromwell Road, SW7 ☎ 0171-938 8500 / 0171-938 8441

⊖ *South Kensington* ◷ *Mon. noon–5.50pm; Tue., Thur.–Sun. 10am–5.50pm; Wed 10am–5.50pm, 6.30–9.30pm● £5; seniors £3; students, children free; White Card* 🏛 ▢ *Victoria & Albert Museum Café* ✖

Founded in 1862, with the aim of inspiring students of design, its galleries, which stretch for seven miles, are filled with extraordinary treasures. The V&A is acknowledged as the world's greatest collection of decorative, fine and applied arts. Take one of the free guided tours. Highlights include the Dress Collection (room 40), the Nehru Gallery of Indian art (room 41) and the Tsui Gallery of Chinese art (room 44) and the superb Glass Gallery (room 131). There's an excellent restaurant in the basement and summer café in the courtyard.

Science Museum (56)
Exhibition Road, SW7 ☎ 0171-938 8080 / 0171-938 8123

⊖ *South Kensington* ◷ *daily 10am–6pm* ● *£5.50; seniors, students, children £2.90; daily after 4.30pm free; White Card*

The Science Museum has five floors packed with discoveries and inventions, with original machines from Stephenson's first steam locomotive (*The Rocket*) to the Apollo 10 space module. Launch Pad is the most popular exhibit for children, with dozens of interactive displays from making soap bubbles to building bridges. The recently refurbished children's basement has attractive displays for the young and very young.

Natural History Museum (57)
Cromwell Road, SW7 ☎ 0171-938 9123

⊖ *South Kensington* ◷ *Mon.–Sat. 10am–5.50pm; Sun. 11am–5.50pm* ● *£6; seniors, students £3.20; children £3; Mon.–Fri. after 4.30pm, Sat. and Sun. after 5pm free; White Card*

The magnificent neo-Gothic building, decorated with hundreds of stone creatures, was opened to the public in 1881. Inside, you can take your pick from Dinosaurs, Discovering Mammals, Creepy Crawlies, Ecology, Evolution, or the Story of Ourselves, or try the Earth Galleries with a journey to the center of the earth to experience the power of volcanoes, earthquakes, glaciers, deserts and tornadoes.

Not forgetting

■ **Albert Memorial (58)** Kensington Gardens (opposite the Royal Albert Hall), SW7 *Striking monument to Prince Albert, Queen Victoria's consort and member of the Great Exhibition committee, who died of typhoid in 1861.*
■ **Royal Albert Hall (59)** Kensington Gore, SW7 ☎ 0171-589 3203 ◷ *daily 9am–9pm Huge, round, red-brick Victorian concert hall, venue for the famous Promenade Concerts* ➡ 88.
■ **Royal College of Art (60)** Kensington Gore, SW7 ☎ 0171-590 4444 ◷ *daily 10am–6pm 1960s seven-story block houses the postgraduate art college. The annual degree shows (May/June) draw large crowds.*

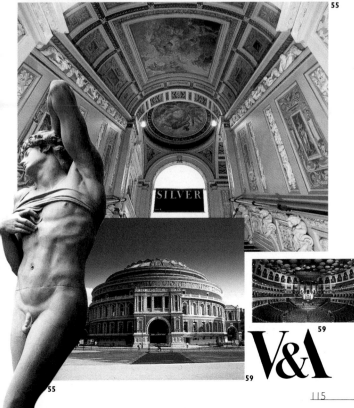

KENSINGTON GARDENS

69   58

The Ring

68   HYDE PARK

Queen's Gate

Alexandra Gate

The Carriage Road

Kensington Gore

Kensington Road

60

21

59

33

ROYAL ALBERT HALL

Prince Consort Road

Exhibition Road

IMPERIAL COLLEGE OF SCIENCE AND TECHNOLOGY

Gate

56

BRITISH MUSEUM OF NATURAL HISTORY

57

VICTORIA AND ALBERT MUSEUM

55

Cromwell Road

Queen's

Queensberry Way

37

Thurloe Place

Thurloe Square

Harrington Road

Thurloe Street

South Kensington

S. Terrace

54

Brompton Road

58

Pelham Street

57

Brompton Road

58

38

Summer Pl.

34

Onslow Square

Pelham Cres. Rd

Fulham Rd

54

58

N

56

58

55

SILVER

55

V&A

59

59

59

In the area

Regent's Park was laid out in the early 19th century as part of the Prince Regent's plans to build a palace on Primrose Hill, with a processional way from The Mall. The palace was never built, but Regent Street, the park and the surrounding Nash Terraces, designed by

What to see

Madame Tussaud's (61)
Marylebone Road, NW1 ☎ 0171-935 6861

⊖ *Baker Street* 🕐 *May–Sep.: daily 9am–5.30pm / Oct.–Apr. : Mon.–Fri. 10am–5.30pm; Sat.–Sun. 9.30am–5.30pm* ● *£8.95; seniors £6.75; children £5.90/ combined ticket with the Planetarium : £11.20; seniors £8.70; children £7.10*

Madame Tussaud emigrated to London from Paris with her waxworks in 1802. This museum, with its wax figures of the famous and infamous, past and present, has now become one of London's most popular tourist attractions. See the chilling Chamber of Horrors and the dark-ride finale called 'The Spirit of London', a 'taxi ride' through London's history.

London Planetarium (62)
Marylebone Road, NW1 ☎ 0171-935 6861

⊖ *Baker Street* 🕐 *June–Aug.: Mon.–Fri. 10.20am–5.20pm; Sat., Sun. 10.40am– 5pm / Sep.–May: Mon.–Fri. 12.20–5pm; Sat., Sun. 10.20am–5pm* ● *£5.65; seniors £4.45; children £3.70 / combined ticket with Madame Tussaud's see above*

The refurbished Planetarium, equipped with a Digistar Mark II projector, the most advanced in the world, allows you to sit back and watch the 30-minute 'Cosmic Perceptions' show. There is also a permanent exhibition on the solar system, space telescopes and weather satellites.

London Zoo (63)
Regent's Park, NW1 ☎ 0171-722 3333

⊖ *Baker Street or Camden Town then 74 bus; by Regent's Canal: take the London Waterbus from Camden Lock or Little Venice ☎ 0171-482 2550* 🅿 🕐 *Mar.– Oct.: daily 10am–4.30pm / Nov.–Feb.: daily 10am–3pm* ● *£8; seniors, students £7; children £6* 💺

This small zoo is world-famous for its conservation activities. It boasts reptile and insect houses, a collection of nocturnal animals (Moonlight House), an aviary designed by Lord Snowdon, and a Children's Zoo. Watch the sealions and penguins feeding, and the elephants' bathtime.

Wallace Collection (64)
Hertford House, Manchester Square, W1 ☎ 0171-935 0687

⊖ *Bond Street* 🕐 *Mon.–Sat. 10am–5pm; Sun. 2–5pm* ● *free*

This magnificent collection of Old Master paintings, furniture, porcelain and armour, bequeathed to the nation by Sir Richard Wallace's widow in 1897, includes works by Rembrandt, Rubens, Titian, Canaletto and Frans Hals (*The Laughing Cavalier*), and renowned 18th-century French paintings by Boucher, Poussin, Watteau and Fragonard. One of the finest small museums in the world.

Not forgetting

■ **Sherlock Holmes Museum (65)** 239 Baker Street, NW1 ☎ 0171-935 8866 🕐 *daily 9.30am–6pm Reconstruction of the fictional detective's lodgings in a Victorian terrace house. On four stories, including living room and dining room. On-site store and restaurant.*

architect John Nash, remain. ■ Where to stay ➧ 38 ■ Where to eat ➧ 74 ■ After dark ➧ 86 ■ What to see ➧ 118

A whole host of stars, past and present, have been immortalized at Madame Tussaud's.

61

Basic facts

In Tudor times, London's central parks were royal hunting grounds. Later monarchs opened up the land to the citizens of London, providing an almost continuous stretch of grass and trees from Horse Guards Parade to Notting Hill Gate, a pleasant walk of about three miles. All the parks

What to see

St James's Park (66)

The Mall, SW1
☎ *0171-930 1793*
🚇 *St James's Park*
♿ 🚻 *Cake House*
🎵 *live bands in summer*

St James's is the oldest of the royal parks. The lake and its islands are a bird sanctuary with over 30 species of waterfowl and several resident pelicans. There is also a small playground and refreshments are available all year round in the Cake House. There are magnificent views of the front of Buckingham

Palace from the bridge across the lake.

Green Park (67)

Constitution Hill, Piccadilly, SW1
☎ *0171-930 1793*
🚇 *Green Park, Hyde Park Corner*

Green Park is a pleasant, shady expanse of grass and trees. The delightful Queen's Walk, with the old gas lamps still in place, runs along the east side of the park from Piccadilly to The Mall. At lunchtimes on fine days, workers and students come here to relax and

take a break from the hustle and bustle of central London.

Hyde Park (68)

Park Lane, Bayswater, Knightsbridge
☎ *0171-298 2100*
🚇 *Hyde Park Corner, Marble Arch, Lancaster Gate, Knightsbridge*
♿ 🚻 *The Dell, The Lido Café*

The largest and best-known of London's central parks, Hyde Park has been open to the public since 1637. You can horseride along Rotten Row, take a rowing boat out

on the lake, swim at the Serpentine Lido or simply relax in a deckchair. There are also four tennis courts on the south side of the park opposite the Albert Memorial. ☎ *0171-262 3474* Visit Hyde Park on a Sunday to hear the soapbox orators at the famous Speakers' Corner, on the north side of the park near Marble Arch.

Kensington Gardens (69)

Bayswater Road, Kensington Road
☎ *0171-724 2826*

67

68

66

66

described below are open daily from sunrise to sunset.

◉ *Lancaster Gate, Queensway* ♿ 🚻 🎎 *The Orangery*

Kensington Gardens, which merge with Hyde Park, were once the private gardens for Kensington Palace (open to visitors). There are formal gardens, shady walks, two playgrounds, and a large stretch of water, the Round Pond, where adults and children alike come to sail model boats. The famous statue of Peter Pan stands near the Long Water.

Holland Park (70)

Abbotsbury Road, Kensington High Street
◉ *Holland Park,*
Kensington High Street ✂ ♿ 🎎
Holland Park Open Air Theatre

This delightful, quiet, and perhaps most romantic of all London's central parks was the private garden for Holland House, once a splendid Jacobean mansion (constructed in 1606). There are formal gardens with peacocks, shady woodland, a peaceful Japanese garden with a stream and waterfalls and a pleasant café. During the summer the Open Air Theatre (0171-603 1123), with protection from an elegant canopy, stages performances of opera, dance and theater.

Regent's Park (71)

Outer Circle
☎ *0171-486 7905*
◉ *Regent's Park, Baker Street* ✂ ♿
🎎 *Regent's Park Open Air Theatre*
☎ *0171-486 2431*

Regent's Park was formerly Henry VIII's royal hunting ground. Nowadays, this popular royal park offers a variety of activities including a large boating lake for adults and a small boating lake for children (complete with canoes and pedalos), a number of public tennis courts, three playgrounds and the world-famous Zoo ➡ 116 in the northeast corner. In summer there's an Open Air Theatre ➡ 86 which performs three shows each year. For horticultural visitors, Queen Mary's Rose Garden is at its best in May and June.

70

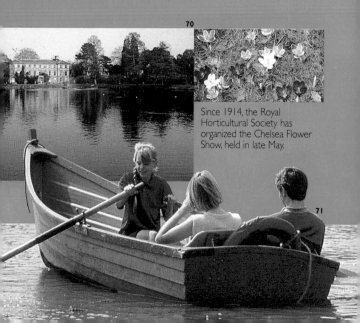

Since 1914, the Royal Horticultural Society has organized the Chelsea Flower Show, held in late May.

71

Further afield

By bus

Buses run by *Green Line* depart from Eccleston Bridge (behind Victoria station) for Hampton Court ➡ 130, Windsor ➡ 132 and several other towns and villages within a radius of around 40 miles of London. *Green Line* ☎ 0171-668 7261

By boat

Westminster Passenger Services ☎ 0171-930 1661 ☎ 0171-930 2062
From Westminster Pier to:
Greenwich ➡ 126, all year round, 50 mins (£4 one-way; £6 roundtrip);
Kew ➡ 128, April to October in 90 mins;
Richmond ➡ 128, April to October in 2 hours;
Hampton Court ➡ 128, April to October in 3 hours.

36
Days out
THE INSIDER'S FAVORITES

Organized tours

For organized tours of Greenwich,
Kew, Richmond, Hampton Court, Windsor
and more, contact:
Evan Evans ☎ 0181-332 2222
Frame Richards ☎ 0171-837 3111
Golden Tours ☎ 0171-233 7030
For tours of some of Britain's finest gardens, May to
October (£49.50 for a whole day).
☎ 0171-720 4891

Basic facts

Some of London's most beautiful attractions are situated along the Thames: Greenwich, Syon Park, Kew Gardens, Hampton Court, Windsor. Some parks and castles are still accessible by boat. Situated on a hill in north London, Hampstead is the most central of these days out.

Further afield

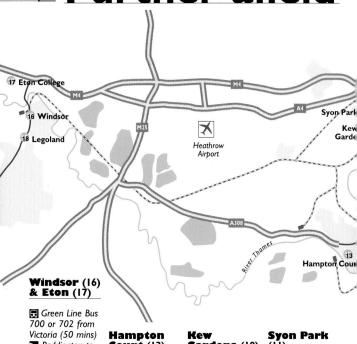

17 Eton College

M4

M4

A4

Syon Park

16 Windsor

M25

Kew Gardens

18 Legoland

✈ Heathrow Airport

A308

River Thames

13 Hampton Court

Windsor (16) & Eton (17)

🚌 Green Line Bus 700 or 702 from Victoria (50 mins)
🚆 Paddington to Windsor and Eton Central (35 mins) or Waterloo to Windsor and Eton Riverside (50 mins) Buses and trains travel into central Windsor.

Hampton Court (13)

🚆 Waterloo to Hampton Court (35 mins)
🚤 Westminster Pier (3 hours) Boat trips April to October.

Kew Gardens (10)

Ⓔ Kew Gardens (15 mins from Earl's Court)
🚤 Westminster Pier (90 mins) Boat trips April to October.

Syon Park (11)

Ⓔ Kew Bridge (15 mins from Earl's Court) then 237 or 267 bus Allow 10 mins walk from Kew to Syon Park.

16

13

4

16

Kenwood House 3

4 **Highgate Cemetary**

2 **Hampstead Heath**

1 **Hampstead Village**

Paddington

Charing Cross

CITY

Waterloo

River Thames

Greenwich 5 9

A406

A41

A40

A4

A2

A3

12 **Richmond Park**

River Thames

Richmond Park (12)

🚇 Richmond (20 mins from Earl's Court)

🚆 Waterloo to Richmond (15 mins)

Take a bus, or even walk (10–15 mins) from Kew Gardens or Syon Park to Richmond Park.

Hampstead Village (1)

🚇 Hampstead

🚆 Hampstead Heath

Most easily reached by tube (15 mins from Charing Cross), which brings you out right in the center of the village.

Kenwood House (3)

🚇 Hampstead or 210 bus from Golders Green or Archway Kenwood stands on the north side of Hampstead Heath.

Hampstead Heath (2)

🚇 Hampstead, Belsize Park, Highgate, Archway

🚆 Gospel Oak or Hampstead Heath then 24, 210 or 271 buses

The Heath is 10 mins walk from Hampstead village.

Highgate Cemetery (4)

🚇 Archway then 210 bus Allow 10 mins on foot from Archway tube station to Highgate cemetery.

Greenwich (5) to (9)

🚆 **Docklands Light Railway** from Bank or Tower Gateway to Island Garden, then take the tunnel under the Thames

🚆 Charing Cross to Greenwich or Maze Hill

⛴ Westminster or Tower Pier to Greenwich Pier (50 mins)

The ferry provides the most pleasant means of traveling to Greenwich. Beware: the last boat back is around 4pm.

1

11

9

These hilltop villages, some four miles northwest of central London, are separated by the expanse of Hampstead Heath. Despite an increasing volume of traffic, both retain 18th-century village charm, with steep, narrow streets, stores, cafés, restaurants and an affluent yet bohemian air.

Further afield

Hampstead Village (1)

⊖ Fenton House *Hampstead Grove, NW3* ☎ *0171-435 3471*
Keats House *Wentworth Place, Keats Grove, NW3* ☎ *0171-435 2062*

The streets of Hampstead are lined with attractive residential buildings. Fenton House, a superb red-brick house and garden (built 1693), has a rich collection of historic musical instruments and stages occasional concerts. Keats House contains letters and other memorabilia relating to the Romantic poet John Keats, who lived here from 1818 to 1820.

Hampstead Heath (2)

A huge wooded heath, with grassy slopes and twelve large ponds. At the south end, from the top of Parliament Hill (a favorite spot for kite-flyers), there are magnificent views over London. There is free swimming in three of the ponds (ladies', men's, and mixed bathing). There are funfairs on public holidays, and at Kenwood House lakeside concerts are held on Saturday evenings throughout the summer.

Kenwood House (3)
Hampstead Lane, NW3 ☎ 0181-348 1286

◔ *Apr.–Oct.: daily 10am–6pm / Nov.–Mar.: daily 10am–4pm* ● *free* ◻ ⊞

The elegant cream-colored mansion on the northern slopes of the Heath, with its superb collection of paintings and furniture, was bequeathed to the nation by Lord Iveagh in 1927. Highlights of the collection include a rare Vermeer (*The Lute Player*), a Rembrandt self-portrait, a Turner seascape and portraits by Gainsborough and Reynolds. The stunning blue-and-gold library is by Robert Adam, the most brilliant designer of his day, who remodeled the house in the 18th century.

Highgate Cemetery (4)
Swain's Lane, N6 ☎ 0181-340 1834

◔ *Eastern Cemetery Apr.–Oct.: daily 10am–5pm / Nov.–Mar.: daily 10am–4pm* ● *£1 Western Cemetery* ▣ *Mon.–Fri. noon, 2pm, 4pm (3pm in winter); Sat.– Sun. every hour from 11am to 4pm (3pm in winter)* ● *£5*

Highgate is famous for its Victorian cemetery. The older West Cemetery is a romantic wilderness of crumbling ornate tombs, stone angels, catacombs and the extraordinary Egyptian Avenue. Chemist and physicist Michael Faraday and poet Christina Rossetti are buried here. The East Cemetery's most celebrated occupant is Karl Marx, whose large and unmistakable bust draws visitors from all over the world.

Not forgetting

■ **Louis Patisserie** 32 Heath Street, Hampstead, NW3 ☎ 0171-435 9908 ◔ *daily 9am–6pm Charming tea rooms with delicious cakes and pastries.*
■ **Brew House** Kenwood House, Hampstead Lane, NW3 ☎ 0181-431 5384 ◔ *Apr.–Oct.: daily 9am–6pm / Nov.–Mar.: 9am–4pm Home-made dishes and pastries.* ■ **Lauderdale Restaurant** Waterlow Park, Highgate Hill, N6 ☎ 0181-341 4807 ◔ *Tue.–Sun. 9am–7pm Restaurant located in a lovely 17th-century building on the edge of Waterlow Park.*

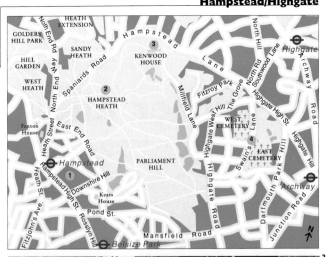

A beautiful garden surrounds the delightful
Kenwood House. Lakeside concerts are held
throughout the summer.

In the area

Henry VIII lived here within sight of the Royal Dockyards. Later, the Royal Observatory, the Royal Naval College and, in 1884, the Greenwich Meridian (from which Greenwich Mean Time is measured) were established here. Greenwich will host Britain's millennium exhibition.

Further afield

Old Royal Observatory (5)
Greenwich Park, at the top of the hill ☎ 0181-858 4422

⊙ *daily 10am–5pm* ● *combined ticket for the Old Royal Observatory, National Maritime Museum and Queen's House £5.50; seniors, students, children £4.50*

Founded by Charles II in 1675, this is where the Royal Astronomer carried out much important research including the calculation of the Zero Meridian. The Observatory holds a collection of clocks, telescopes and navigational instruments. Greenwich Mean Time is measured from here.

Greenwich Park (6)

Roman and Saxon remains have been discovered here, but this riverside park (the oldest of the royal parks) takes its shape from Tudor and Stuart times. Henry VIII was born here, and it was one of his favorite residences. The view from the top of the hill is spectacular.

Queen's House (7)
Greenwich Park, SE10 ☎ 0181-858 4422

⊙ *daily 10am–5pm* ● *combined ticket (see above)*

The first Palladian-style house to be seen in Britain, designed in 1616 by Inigo Jones for James I's wife, Anne of Denmark. Christopher Wren later designed many of the buildings still to be seen in Greenwich. Queen's House has beeen refurbished in its original 17th-century colors.

National Maritime Museum (8)
Romney Road, SE10 ☎ 0181-858 4422

⊙ *daily 10am–5pm* ● *combined ticket (see above)*

The museum of Britain's seafaring history is housed in several buildings around Greenwich Park. The East and West wings give the history of boat building, merchant ships, the navy and great explorers, with a superb collection of real and model ships.

Cutty Sark and Gipsy Moth IV (9)
King William Walk, SE10 ☎ 0181-858 3445

⊙ *Cutty Sark May–Sep.: Mon.–Sat. 10am–6pm; Sun. noon–6pm / Oct.–Apr.: Mon.–Sat. 10am–5pm; Sun. noon–5pm* ● *£3.50; seniors, children £2.50* **Gipsy Moth IV** *daily 10am–5pm* ● *£1*

Built in Scotland in 1869, the *Cutty Sark* is the last and the fastest of the three-masted clippers, which once sailed to China and Australia to bring back cargoes of tea and wool. Her figurehead shows a witch in her 'cutty sark' (Scottish dialect for 'short shift'). Nearby is the *Gipsy Moth IV*, in which Sir Francis Chichester sailed single-handed around the world (1966–67).

Not forgetting

■ **Trafalgar Tavern** Park Row, SE10 ☎ 0181-293 3337 ⊙ *daily 11.30am–11pm Tavern built in 1837. Good fried fish and a view of the Thames.*

Where to shop
➡ 161

In the area

Richmond has something of the air of a small country town, especially in the small streets around Richmond Green (once the site of Henry VII's Tudor palace) and near the bridge (the oldest in London, dating from 1774). Nearby Kew is world-famous for its botanical gardens and

 # Further afield

Kew Palace & Gardens (10)
Kew Road, Richmond, Surrey ☎ 0181-332 5622 / 0181-940 1171

◐ *Palace* reopening in 1998, for information call ☎ 0181-781 9500
Gardens daily 9.30am to sundown **Orchid festival** Feb. 14.–Mar. 31 ● £4.50; seniors £3, students, children £2.50

First planted in the 1760s for Princess Augusta and later enhanced by exotic specimens brought back by Sir Joseph Banks from his round-the-world voyages with Captain Cook, the Royal Botanic Gardens started life as the private gardens for Kew Palace. In 1841 the gardens, made up of acres of shady woodland walks, lakes and planted areas, were given to the state. There are also giant glasshouses (Palm House, Temperate House and Princess of Wales House). Hidden among the greenery are the ten-story pagoda and Queen Charlotte's Thatched Cottage. This red-brick, Dutch-style house, built in 1631, is the smallest of the royal palaces and was used by George III, Queen Charlotte and their 13 children as a summer home. The garden is planted in 17th-century style with lavender, rosemary and bergamot surrounded by box hedges.

Syon Park & House (11)
London Road, Brentford ☎ 0181-560 0881

◐ *Gardens* daily 10am–6pm ● £2.50 *Palace* Apr.–Sep.: Tue.–Sun. 11am–5pm; Oct.–Dec.: Sun. 11am–5pm ● £5.50 (palace and gardens)

On the opposite bank from Kew, the Duke of Northumberland's 16th-century mansion house, refurbished in the 1760s, has an immense gallery adorned with paintings by Zuccarelli and furniture by Robert Adam. The grounds include a rose garden, a conservatory and a butterfly house.

Richmond Park (12)
Richmond, Surrey ☎ 0181-948 3209

◐ 24-hour access to pedestrians; cars 7.30am–sundown ● free

This former royal hunting ground is now one of the largest city parks in Europe. The expanse of open grassland and woodland is home to herds of red and fallow deer, and to other wildlife including foxes and badgers. In May and June, the Isabella plantation has a superb display of rhododendrons and azaleas. White Lodge, once a royal hunting lodge, houses the junior branch of the Royal Ballet School. From the top of Richmond Hill and the nearby Pembroke Lodge, there is a famous view over the Thames, painted by both Turner and Constable.

Not forgetting

■ **Ham House** Ham Street, Richmond ☎ 0181-940 1950 ◐ Apr.–Oct.: Sat.–Wed. 11am–5pm *17th-century house and gardens. Tea rooms in the Orangery.* ■ **Maids of Honour** 288 Kew Road, Kew ☎ 0181-940 2752 ◐ Mon. 9.30am–1pm; Tue.–Sat. 9.30am–6pm *Tea rooms serving the famous 'maids of honour' cakes – once a favorite with Henry VIII.* ■ **Hothouse** 9 Station Approch, Kew ☎ 0181-332 1923 ◐ daily 10am–7pm *Delicious snacks, near Kew Gardens station.* ■ **Café Mozart** 4 Church Court, Richmond ☎ 0181-940 2014 ◐ daily 9am–7pm *Friendly café in the heart of Richmond.*

tropical
glasshouses.

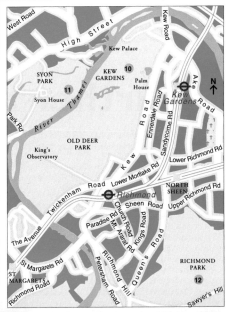

The glasshouses at
Kew display an
extraordinary range of
plants from around the
world.

ROYAL
BOTANIC
GARDENS
KEW

10

11

10 11

In the area

This magnificent Tudor palace, with additions by Christopher Wren, was first opened to the public by Queen Victoria in 1838. Parts of the palace are now used as residences for retired servants from the royal household. Visit during the Summer Music Festival (in June) and Flower

Further afield

Hampton Court Palace (13)
East Molesey, Surrey ☎ 0181-781 9500

🕐 *Apr.–Oct.: Mon. 10.15am–6pm;Tue.–Sun. 9.30am–6pm / Oct.–Mar.: Mon. 10.15am–4.30pm;Tue.–Sun. 9.30am–4.30pm* ● *combined ticket with the park £8; seniors, students £5.75; children £4.90*

Hampton Court, built by Cardinal Wolsey between 1514 and 1520, was taken over by Henry VIII in 1529. Henry enlarged the kitchens and rebuilt the Great Hall with a magnificent hammerbeam roof. In 1689, William and Mary commissioned Christopher Wren to modernize the palace, particularly the King's and Queen's apartments around Fountain Court, introducing the Renaissance style. The Astronomical Clock (1540), on the gatehouse leading to Clock Court, shows the time of high tide at London Bridge as well as the hour, day, month and phases of the moon. This proved useful when the Thames was the main highway to Westminster and the City, and the king and his courtiers were rowed here in the royal barge. A guided tour includes the State apartments, the Tudor kitchens where banquets were prepared, the Hall and Chapel, and the Haunted Gallery (purportedly haunted by the ghost of Catherine Howard). Don't miss Mantegna's *The Triumph of Caesar* bought by Charles I.

The Gardens and Maze (14)

🕐 *Park daily, sunrise to sunset* ● *combined ticket with the palace (see above)* *Maze Mar.–Oct.* ● *£1.70; children £1 Flower Festival mid-July.* ● *£17*

With the Thames on one side, the gardens extend all around the palace. The Privy Garden, to the south, has recently been restored to its formal 17th-century style, with a wrought-iron screen at the river end by Jean Tijou (whose work can also be seen in St Paul's Cathedral). The small Banqueting House on the riverside was built by Christopher Wren. Further west, you can see the Great Vine, the oldest known vine in the world, planted in 1768 by landscape gardener 'Capability' Brown, and still producing around 600lbs of grapes every year. The Fountain Garden and Broad Walk extend along the east front of the palace, with the Tudor Tennis Court (Henry VIII was a keen player). North of the palace, past the Wilderness and the Tiltyard Gardens, is the Maze, laid out in 1714.

Bushy Park (15)

Just north of the Maze, beyond the Lion Gates, Bushy Park is a peaceful expanse of wooded parkland, with ornamental ponds, herds of deer, and Wren's famous mile-long avenue of chestnut trees, a breathtaking sight in May when covered with pink and white blossoms.

Not forgetting

■ **Tiltyard Tearoom** Hampton Court Palace ☎ 0181-943 3666 🕐 *summer: daily 10am–5pm; winter: daily 10am–4pm Tea rooms on the site of Henry VIII's former tournament grounds. Hot food, salads and desserts. Garden terrace open in summer.*

Festival (in early July). Allow half a day to explore the house and gardens.

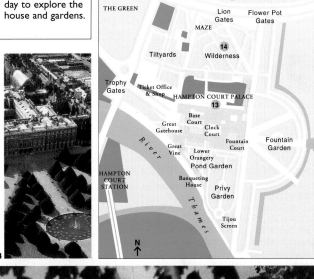

15 BUSHY PARK

THE GREEN

Lion Gates
Flower Pot Gates

MAZE

14 Wilderness

Tiltyards

Trophy Gates

Ticket Office & Shop

HAMPTON COURT PALACE

13

Great Gatehouse

Base Court

Clock Court

Fountain Court

Fountain Garden

Great Vine

Lower Orangery

Pond Garden

HAMPTON COURT STATION

Banqueting House

Privy Garden

Tijou Screen

River Thames

N

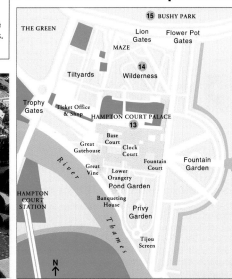

14

13

14

13

The small town of Windsor is overshadowed by the impressive bulk of Windsor Castle, standing on a hill overlooking the Thames. The attractive old town, with cobbled streets, Georgian houses, and a Guildhall designed by Christopher Wren, is always crowded with

Further afield

Windsor Castle (16)
Castle Hill, Windsor ☎ (01753) 868286

◐ *Mar.–Oct.: daily 10am–4pm / Nov.–Feb.: daily 10am–3pm* **Changing of the guard** *May–Aug.: Mon.–Sat. 11am / Sep.–Apr.: Mon.–Sat. alternate days 11am (check beforehand)* ● *£9.80; seniors £7.20; children £5.60 (including Doll's House)*

This is the oldest of the royal residences, inhabited almost continuously since the 11th century. The original wooden keep, erected after the Norman invasion of 1066, was rebuilt in stone during the reign of Henry II (1154–89). The round tower and battlements were repaired in the 18th century by George IV. The state apartments, badly damaged in a disastrous fire in 1992, have now reopened. Highlights of a tour here are the exquisite Queen Mary's Dolls House, designed by architect Edwin Lutyens, and St George's Chapel (1475–1528), a glorious example of Perpendicular Gothic architecture, with a fan-vaulted ceiling to rival the Henry VII Chapel at Westminster. Henry VIII lies among the Royal Tombs here. As at Buckingham Palace, the royal standard flies over the castle when the Queen is in residence.

Eton College (17)
Eton, Berkshire ☎ (01753) 671177

◐ *Easter, Jul.–Aug.: daily 10.30am–4.30pm / Easter–Jun., Sep.: daily 2pm–4.30pm* ● *£2.50; children £2* ▣ *2.15pm and 3.30pm* ● *£3.50*

England's most famous and exclusive school was founded in 1440 by Henry VI for 70 poor scholars. School uniform is black tailcoats and striped trousers. Take a guided tour to see the college buildings, including the 15th-century graffiti-encrusted Lower School schoolroom and the splendid fan-vaulted perpendicular chapel, with its original medieval wall paintings.

Legoland (18)
Windsor Park, Windsor ☎ (0990) 626375 / (0990) 070809

◐ *Apr.–mid-July: daily 10am–6pm / mid-July–Aug.: daily 10am–8pm / mid-July–Sep.: daily 10am–6pm / Oct.: Sat., Sun. 10am–6pm* ● *£15; children £12*

This popular theme park (mainly for 5–12-year-olds) is on the site of the former Windsor Safari Park. The main attraction is Miniland, reached by a funicular railway, with a reconstruction of familiar sights (Big Ben, Tower Bridge) from Britain, Italy, Germany and Denmark, all built from Lego bricks. The rest of the park is made up of fairground rides.

Not forgetting

■ **Adam & Eve Pub** 29 Thames Street, Windsor ☎ (01753) 864359 ◐ *Mon.–Sat. 11am–11pm; Sun. 11am–10.30pm Pub right in the heart of Windsor, near the theater. Good hot food served at lunchtime and in the evenings.* ■ **Waterside Inn** Ferry Road, Bray-on-Thames, Maidenhead, Berkshire ☎ (01628) 20691 ◐ *Tue. 7–11pm; Wed.–Sat. noon–2.30pm, 7–11pm; Sun. 7–11pm Large French restaurant to the west of Windsor Castle (15 mins by car).*

tourists. On the opposite bank of the Thames, Eton is generally much less crowded and the famous College is open to visitors in the afternoons.

Several regiments guard Windsor and Queen Elizabeth II all year round.

Basic facts

Football and rugby attract thousands of fans during the winter months, but summer is when the majority of important sporting events take place. Reserve well in advance: seats for major events can be difficult to get hold of. For up-to-date information see the Sports section of *Time*

▶ Further afield

Stadiums

Wembley (19)

Empire Way, Wembley HA9 0DJ
☎ *0181-900 1234 or 0181-902 8833*
🚇 *Wembley Park*
🕐 *daily 10am– 4pm (except on match days)* ●
£6.95 Built for the Empire Games in 1924, this 80,000-seater stadium in northwest London is the UK's most famous sports arena. Football internationals, the FA Cup Final, the Rugby League Challenge Cup and other important matches are played here. Greyhound racing is held on Mon., Wed. and Fri.

Guided tours include a movie of Wembley's historic moments.

Crystal Palace (20)

Ledrington Road, SE19
☎ *0181-778 0131*
🚇 *Victoria to Crystal Palace*
Some of the most important athletics competitions in Britain are held here.

Cricket

Lord's (21)

St John's Wood Road, NW8
☎ *0171-289 1611*
🚇 *St John's Wood*
🕐 *daily noon, 2pm (except on match days)*
● *£5.50*
☎ *0171-432 1033*
The most famous cricket venue in England hosts at least one international match each year. Middlesex County play here and it is home to the all-male Marylebone Cricket Club (MCC), founded in 1787. The small museum charts the history of the club and the game.

Golf

Two 18-hole championship-class golf courses, on the circuit for inter-national events.

Sunningdale (27)

Ridgemount Road, Sunningale, Berkshire SL5 9RR
☎ *(01344) 21681*
🚉 *Waterloo to Sunningale*

Wentworth (28)

Wentworth Drive, Virginia Water, Surrey JU25 4LS
☎ *(01344) 842201*
🚉 *Waterloo to Virginia Water*
Volvo PGA Championship is held here in May.

Out magazine or call Sportsline ☎ 0171-222 8000.

Football

Season runs mid-August to May. Five London clubs play in the FA Carling Premiership League.

Arsenal (22)
Avenell Road, Highbury, N5
☎ 0171-704 4000
🚇 Arsenal

Chelsea (23)
Stamford Bridge, Fulham Road, SW6
☎ 0171-385 5545
🚇 Fulham Broadway

Tottenham Hotspur (24)
White Hart Lane, 748 High Rd, N17
☎ 0181-365 5000
🚇 Wood Green

West Ham United (25)
Boleyn Ground, Green Street, Upton Park E13 9AZ
☎ 0181-548 2700
🚇 Upton Park

Wimbledon (26)
Selhurst Park, Park Road, SE25
☎ 0181-771 2233
🚆 Victoria to Selhurst

Horse racing

Ascot (29)
Ascot, Berkshire SL5 7JN
☎ (01344) 22211
🚆 Waterloo to Ascot
Over 20 flat races and jumps races with the Royal Meeting (usually third week of June)

as the year's highlight.

Epsom (30)
Epsom Downs, Surrey
☎ (01372) 470047
🚆 Waterloo to Epsom
The Oaks and the Derby, early June, are the two famous classics.

Sandown Park (31)
Portsmouth Road, Esher, Surrey
☎ (01372) 470047
🚆 Waterloo to Esher
An annual program of around 25 flat and jumps races.

Kempton Park (32)
Sunbury-on-Thames, Middlesex
☎ (01372) 470047
🚆 Waterloo to Kempton Park
The closest racecourse to central London. A program of popular summer evening meetings.

Windsor (33)
Maidenhead Road, Windsor, Berks
☎ (01753) 865234
Pleasant Thames-side setting, with summer evening meetings (flat and jumps racing).

Tennis

Queen's Club (34)
Pallister Road, W14
☎ 0171-385 3421
🚇 Barons Court
The Stella Artois Championship is held here in mid-June in the run-up to Wimbledon.

All England Club (35)
Church Road, SW19
🚇 Southfields
☎ 0181-946 2244
🏛 Museum: Tue.–Sat. 10.30am–5pm; Sun. 2–5pm
● £2.50
☎ 0181-946 6131
Venue for the Wimbledon Championships, (last week of June and first

week of July).The museum has videos of past championships and memorabilia of tennis stars, past and present.

Rugby

Twickenham (36)
Rugby Road, Twickenham TW1 1DZ
☎ 0181-892 8161
🚆 Waterloo to Twickenham
🏛 Museum: Tue.–Sat. 10.30am–5pm; Sun. 2–5pm
● £2.50 🏛 £4
☎ 0181-892 2000
The venue for England's international fixtures and all-important games and cup finals. There are guided tours of the stadium, and the small museum tells the history of the game.

CAMBRIDGE

Where to find what
Books in Charing Cross Road;
hi-fi equipment on Tottenham
Court Road and Denmark Street;
department stores around
Knightsbridge; fashion and gifts in
Covent Garden; tailors in Savile
Row and Jermyn Street.

Where to shop

Conversions
Weights
ounce = 28g
pound = 453g
Measures
inch = 2.54cms
foot = 30.48cms
Liquids
pint = 0.57 liter
gallon = 4.5 liters

Women
Clothes sizes
US 8 = UK 10
US 10 = UK 12
US 12 = UK 14
Shoe sizes
US 6½ = UK 5
US 7½ = UK 6
US 8½ = UK 7

Men
Clothes sizes
UK and US jacket,
trousers and shirt sizes
are the same.
Shoe sizes
US 8 = UK 8½
US 9 = UK 9½
US 10 = UK 10½

Sales

In London the Christmas sales begin in late December/early January and the summer sales run throughout July.

Tax

Visitors to the UK can reclaim any VAT (Value Added Tax) they have had to pay. Some major stores operate a scheme whereby you can reclaim VAT in the store itself.

77 Shops

THE INSIDER'S FAVORITES

Basic facts

The development of the department store in the late 19th century revolutionized Londoners' shopping. Many famous stores – Harrods, Harvey Nichols, John Lewis, Liberty – date from this period. The 'modern' department stores, aiming to cater for all shoppers' needs, began when

► **Where to shop**

Harrods (1)
87–135 Brompton Road, SW1 ☎ 0171-730 1234 ➡ 0171-581 0470

⊖ *Knightsbridge* 🕓 *Mon., Tue., Sat. 10am–6pm; Wed.–Fri. 10am–7pm* ▱

London's most famous department store offers an unparalleled range of goods (everything from thimbles to suits of armor), and no fewer than 12 eating and drinking options including a sushi bar and a pizzeria.

Harvey Nichols (2)
109–125 Knightsbridge, SW1 ☎ 0171-235 5000 ➡ 0171-259 6084

⊖ *Knightsbridge* 🕓 *Mon.–Tue., Thur.–Fri. 10am–7pm; Wed. 10am–8pm; Sat. 10am–6pm; Sun. noon–5pm* ▱ 🍴 *Fifth Floor* ➡ *60, The Foundation*

Harrods may be the best known, but Harvey Nichols is the most elegant department store in town, thanks largely to its superb selection of fashion labels and innovations such as the Art Supermarket where shoppers can buy packaged original artworks off the rack.

John Lewis (3)
278–306 Oxford Street, W1 ☎ 0171-629 7711 ➡ 0171-629 0849

⊖ *Oxford Circus* 🕓 *Mon., Wed., Fri. 9.30am–6pm; Thur. 10am–8pm; Sat. 9am–6pm* ▱ 🏠 *Peter Jones, Sloane Square, SW1 ☎ 0171-730 3434*

John Lewis famously guarantees to be 'never knowingly undersold', meaning that prices here are the keenest in the capital. Recommended for household, electrical and electronic goods.

Gordon
Selfridge
opened an
Oxford Street
store in 1909.

SELFRIDGES **Selfridge's** (4)
400 Oxford Street, W1 ☎ 0171-629 1234 ➡ 0171-495 8321

🔵 *Bond Street* 🕐 *Mon.–Wed., Sat. 9.30am–7pm; Thur., Fri. 9.30am–8pm; Sun. noon–6pm* 🔲

An Oxford Street stalwart that's more stylish and contemporary than most of its neighbors. Selfridge's is particularly strong on designer clothes, cosmetics and international foods.

Marks & Spencer (5)
458 Oxford Street, W1 ☎ 0171-935 7954 ➡ 0171-486 5379

🔵 *Marble Arch, Bond Street* 🕐 *Mon.–Tue., Sat. 9am–7pm; Tue.–Fri. 9am–8pm, Sun. noon–6pm* 🔲 🔣 ☎ *0171-935 4422*

Many British women buy their underwear at M&S and many swear by their rather expensive ready-prepared meals and upmarket sandwiches. Clothing styles are rarely daring but the newer, more experimental lines are stocked at this branch.

MARKS & SPENCER

Liberty (6)
214 Regent Street, W1 ☎ 0171-734 1234 ➡ 0171-573 9876

🔵 *Oxford Circus* 🕐 *Mon., Tue., Fri., Sat. 10am–6.30pm; Thur. 10am–7.30pm; Sun. noon–6pm* 🔲

Housed in a mock-Tudor building, Liberty is known for its trademark prints and fabrics. It is also an excellent source of women's fashions and jewelry, both traditional and modern.

In the area

Once home to a fruit and vegetable market, Covent Garden is one of London's most vibrant shopping districts. A maze of store-lined streets radiate out from the central Piazza, with its boutiques, cafés, crafts market and street entertainers. ■ Where to stay ➡ 18 ■ Where to eat ➡ 44

Where to shop

James Smith & Sons (7)
Hazelwood House, 53 New Oxford Street, WC1 ☎ 0171-836 4731

🚇 Tottenham Court Road *Walking sticks and umbrellas* 🕐 *Mon.–Fri. 9.30am–5.25pm; Sat. 10am–5.25pm*

A traditional maker of high-quality umbrellas. The business was founded in 1830 and has changed little since it moved to this site in 1857. Stock is displayed on racks from which you can pick up a standard umbrella for around £30, or have one made-to-measure. There is also a range of walking sticks (which can also be cut to length) and parasols.

Space NK Apothecary (8)
Thomas Neal's Centre, 37 Earlham Street, WC2 ☎ 0171-379 7030

🚇 Covent Garden *Women's ready-to-wear, accessories, beauty products* 🕐 *Mon.–Sat. 11am–7pm* 🚇 *Unit 7 Bishopsgate Arcade, 135 Bishopsgate, EC2 ☎ 0171-256 2303; 45–47 Brook Street, W1 ☎ 0171-355 1727*

Nicola Kinnaird is the NK in Space NK and her spacious store in Thomas Neal's Centre is a heaven for style-seekers. Her fashions and accessories include Hervé Chapelier bags, Opex watches, All Saints jumpers in autumnal shades. The Apothecary section, a wonderful range of cult make-up and toiletry from names such as Kiehls and François Nars, has been so successful that it has spawned branches of its own.

Paul Smith (9)
40–44 Floral Street, WC2 ☎ 0171-379 7133

🚇 Covent Garden *Ready-to-wear for men, women and children* 🕐 *Mon.–Wed., Fri. 10.30am–6.30pm; Thur. 10.30am–7pm; Sat. 10am–6pm* 🚇 *23 Avery Row, W1 ☎ 0171-493 1287*

Paul Smith has been one of the great successes of the British fashion scene and even had an exhibition devoted to him at London's Design Museum ➡ 98. There is a 1960s and 1970s influence in his menswear, and his modern tailoring and striking textiles have made his women's and children's wear and accessories very sought-after. End of line items are sold off at his branch at 23 Avery Row.

Ted Baker (10)
1–3 Langley Court, WC2 ☎ 0171-497 8862

🚇 Covent Garden *Sportswear* 🕐 *Mon.–Wed., Fri. 10am–7pm; Thur. 10am–7.30pm; Sat. 10am–6.30pm; Sun. noon–5pm* 🚇 *7 Fouberts Place, W1 ☎ 0171-437 5619*

Ted Baker is one of the hottest names in men's shirts for clubbers and hip young things. Unusual fabrics are a specialty, so if you are looking for silky ultra-lightness, shiny plastics or furry decadence, then Ted is your man. The T-shirt range is a big seller and there are also jackets and jeans.

Not forgetting

■ **Red or Dead (11)** Thomas Neal's Centre, 37 Earlham Street, WC2 ☎ 0171-240 5576 *Shoes and clubwear.* ■ **Dr Martens (12)** 1–4 King Street, WC2 ☎ 0171-497 1460 *Famous hardwearing shoes plus clothes.*

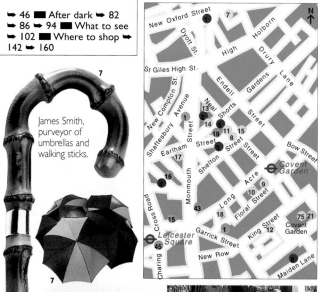

7

James Smith, purveyor of umbrellas and walking sticks.

7

7

9

12

12

In the area

Alongside the many clothes stores in Covent Garden are specialty stores selling some of the best teas and cheeses in Britain. ■ Where to stay ➡ 18 ■ Where to eat ➡ 44 ➡ 46 ■ After dark ➡ 82 ➡ 86 ➡ 90 ➡ 94 ■ What to see ➡ 102 ■ Where to shop ➡ 140 ➡ 160

Where to shop

Neal's Yard Remedies (13)
15 Neal's Yard, WC2 ☎ 0171-379 7222 ➡ 0171-379 0705

⊖ Covent Garden **Natural beauty products and herbal remedies** 🕒 Mon.–Fri. 10am–6pm; Sat. 10am–5.30pm; Sun. 11am–5pm ▭ ♦♦ Chelsea Farmer's Market, Sydney Street, SW3 ☎ 0171-351 6380; 9 Elgin Crescent, W11 ☎ 0171-727 3998; 68 Chalk Farm Road, NW1 ☎ 0171-284 2039

Traditional herbal remedies and cruelty-free, environmentally-friendly cosmetics have proved so popular that branches have also opened in Manchester and Bristol. There is seaweed shampoo, geranium and orange soap, camomile cleanser and fennel toothpaste, along with a superb range of over 200 dried herbs. The staff can advise on the best use of herbal tinctures such as Black Pepper and Myrrh.

Neal's Yard Dairy (14)
17 Shorts Gardens, WC2 ☎ 0171-379 7646 ➡ 0171-240 2442

⊖ Covent Garden **Cheeses** 🕒 Mon.–Sat. 9am–7pm; Sun. 10am–5pm ▭

This wonderful store may be tiny but, since it opened in 1979, it has stimulated a resurgence of interest in British and Irish farmhouse cheeses. Visitors can sample the cheeses, many of which are matured in the store's cellars. The stock varies depending on the season, but usually includes classics such as Appleby's Cheshire, the gouda-like Teifi from Wales, and the creamy, tangy Cashel Blue from Ireland.

Muji (15)
39–41 Shelton Street, WC2 ☎ 0171-379 1331 ➡ 0171-379 1603

⊖ Covent Garden **Household goods and clothes** 🕒 Mon.–Wed., Sat. 10.30am–7pm; Thur., Fri. 10.30am–7.30pm; Sun. noon–6pm ▭ ♦♦ 157 Kensington High Street, W8 ☎ 0171-376 2484; 26 Great Marlborough Street, W1 ☎ 0171-494 1197; 77 King's Road, SW3 ☎ 0171-352 7148

Japanese store Muji's 'no-brand' goods are eco-friendly, minimalist and stylish. Their range of household items includes clothes, accessories and snacks. Plastic, aluminum, wood and cardboard are the dominant materials; mainly in silver, black, gray and white.

R. Twining & Co (16)
216 Strand, WC2 ☎ 0171-353 3511

⊖ Temple **Teas and coffees** 🕒 Mon.–Fri. 9.30am–4.30pm ▭

This narrow, corridor-like store is almost 300 years old and celebrates Twining's long history as tea shippers. Paintings of eminent family members line the walls above racks of teas which range from the classic Earl Grey to more modern herbal and fruit infusions. At the back of the store is a small museum dedicated to the history of the company.

Not forgetting

■ **The Wild Bunch (17)** 22 Earlham Street, WC2 ☎ 0171-497 1200 *Friendly street seller, range of flowers.* ■ **Stanford's (18)** 12–14 Long Acre, WC2 ☎ 0171-836 1915 *Modern and reproduction maps plus travel books.*

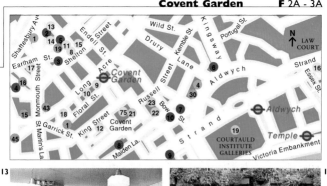

Muji, which means 'no name' in Japanese, carries an ever-increasing range of articles for the home, clothes and accessories.

TWININGS

In the area

The maze of streets bounded by Regent Street, Oxford Street, Charing Cross Road and Shaftesbury Avenue is one of London's most diverse shopping areas. Soho is packed with unusual small stores.
■ Where to stay ➡ 18 ■ Where to eat ➡ 48 ■ After dark ➡ 90

 # Where to shop

Contemporary Ceramics (19)
William Blake House, 7 Marshall Street, W1
☎ 0171-437 7605 ➡ 0171-437 7605

❸ Oxford Circus *Ceramics, luxury gifts* 🕐 *Mon.–Wed., Fri., Sat. 10am–5.30pm; Thur. 10am–7pm* ▱

This gallery store carries a selection of work from members of the British Craft Potters' Association. Styles range from Martin Booth's beautifully colored sculptural abstracts to Tony Gant's mugs, jugs and vases. Prices are very reasonable with some pieces costing under £10.

Milroy's of Soho (20)
3 Greek Street, W1 ☎ 0171-437 9311 ➡ 0171-437 1345

❸ Tottenham Court Rd *Whiskey* 🕐 *Mon.–Fri. 10am–7pm; Sat. 10am–6pm* ▱

The best range of whiskeys in London. There are bourbons and Irish whiskey, even Welsh and English whiskeys, but single malts are the specialty. The selection of around 300 malts draws from almost every distillery from the Lowlands to the Orkneys. Prices range from around £15 to over £6,000 for a 50-year-old Glenfiddich. Many whiskeys are available as miniatures (5cl) and Milroy's also stocks whiskey liqueurs and books.

Simply Sausages (21)
93 Berwick Street, W1 ☎ 0171-287 3482

❸ Piccadilly Circus, Oxford Circus, Tottenham Court Road, Leicester Square *Sausages* 🕐 *Mon.–Sat. 9am–6pm* ▱ ▥ *34 Strutton Ground, SW1* ☎ 0171-976 7430; Harts Corner, EC1 ☎ 0171-329 3227

This store changed the way Londoners think about the British banger. A high meat content means that their products are quality fare. The range of over 40 varieties (including seven vegetarian sausages) includes the classic John Nott's sausage (a recipe dating from 1720), the fiery Algerian Merguez and luxury venison and wild mushroom sausage.

Foyles (22)
13–119 Charing Cross Road, WC2 ☎ 0171-437 5660

❸ Tottenham Court Road *Bookstore* 🕐 *Mon.–Wed., Fri.–Sat. 9am–6pm; Thur. 9am–7pm* ▱

This idiosyncratic bookstore carries paperback fiction arranged by publisher rather than author, and the unusual system of having to collect your check from one desk and pay at another. Don't be put off by the apparent mess – Foyles does have a huge stock and its specialist departments contain many rare editions.

Not forgetting

■ **Lina Stores (23)** 18 Brewer Street, W1 ☎ 0171-437 6482 *A classic Soho Italian deli with a fine range of home-made pasta.* ■ **Anything Left Handed (24)** 57 Brewer Street, W1 ☎ 0171-437 3910 *Products designed specifically for left-handers.* ■ **Just Games (25)** 71 Brewer Street, W1 ☎ 0171-437 0761 *Traditional and modern board games.*

➡ 92 ➡ 94
■ Where to
shop ➡ 160

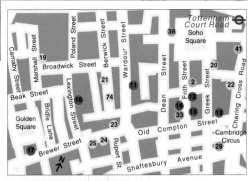

The diverse
range of stores
in Soho makes it
the place to buy
both some of the
best whiskey and
the best sausages
in London.

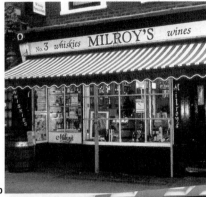

In the area

Elegant Regent Street is the central axis of shoppers' London, with stores ranging from the chains of Oxford Street to the traditional shopping emporia of Piccadilly. It divides the cult boutiques of Soho from the upmarket tailors and antique dealers of Mayfair. ■ Where to eat ➡

Where to shop

Hamleys (26)
188–196 Regent Street, W1 ☎ 0171-734 3161 ➡ 0171-494 5858

⊖ Oxford Circus **Games and toys** 🕐 Mon.–Wed., Fri. 10am–7pm; Thur. 10am–8pm; Sat. 9.30am–7pm; Sun. noon–6pm ▫ ▫ ▯ Unit 3, The Market, Covent Garden Piazza, WC2 ☎ 0171-240 4646

The largest and most famous toy store in London fully justifies its good reputation. Five floors (plus a café and video games arcade in the basement) are packed with shoppers, staff demonstrating the latest crazes, and a huge selection of models, art and craft equipment, dolls, puzzles, sporting goods, books, board games and computer games. The soft toy department offers everything from a superb collection of teddy bears to near life-size giraffes and bears.

Past Times (27)
155 Regent Street, W1 ☎ 0171-734 3728

⊖ Piccadilly Circus, Oxford Circus **Jewelry, luxury gifts** 🕐 Mon.–Wed., Fri., Sat. 9.30am–6pm; Thur. 9.30am–7pm; Sun. 11am–5pm ▫ ▯ The Market, Covent Garden Piazza, WC2 ☎ 0171-240 9265; 179–181 Kensington High Street, W8 ☎ 0171-795 6344; 146 Brompton Road, SW3 ☎ 0171-581 7616

Nostalgia is the driving force behind this chain selling reproduction jewelry, gifts and items inspired by Britain's past. Celtic pins, Saxon amber earrings, Roman games, Medieval gargoyle bookends, Tudor church music, Victorian soaps. Some items are tacky, and some tasteful, but this store is fun if you are not too concerned with authenticity ('Roman' party crackers?). Gift ideas include Victorian nightshirts and tea towels featuring a Rennie Mackintosh design.

Garrard (28)
112 Regent Street, W1 ☎ 0171-734 7020 ➡ 0171-734 0711

⊖ Piccadilly Circus **Jewelry** 🕐 Mon., Wed.–Sat. 9.30am–5.30pm, Tue. 10am–5.30pm ▫

A uniformed doorman ushers customers into the plush, hushed interior of Garrard. The store's atmosphere is as much of an attraction as the classic English jewelry and silverware it sells. Quality is exemplary and prices are steep, as befits a company proudly billing itself as 'the Crown Jeweller'. Garrard was founded in 1735 and prides itself on its commissioning service – if you have the money, they can make almost any item you can think of. There are also clocks, watches and glassware.

Not forgetting

■ **Crabtree & Evelyn (29)** 239 Regent Street, W1 ☎ 0171-409 1603 *Traditional perfumes and toiletries.* ■ **Church's (30)** 201 Regent Street, W1 ☎ 0171-734 2438 *Boots and shoes in a classic-English style.* ■ **The Pen Shop (31)** 199 Regent Street, W1 ☎ 0171-734 4088 *Fountains, ballpoints, engraving and repairs.* ■ **Burberry's (32)** 165 Regent Street, W1 ☎ 0171-734 4060 *Specializes in high-quality waterproof coats.* ■ **Tower Records (33)** 1 Piccadilly Circus, W1 ☎ 0171-439 2500 *Vast range of music, videos and computer games.*

48 ➡ 52 ■ After dark ➡ 86 ➡ 90
■ What to see ➡ 104 ■ Where to shop
➡ 138

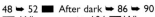

28   31

29

30

26

29

32

Hamleys

In the area

Nowhere in London is an area's history more reflected in its stores than St James's. Even today the modern gent can find top-quality luxury stores on his club's doorstep. ■ Where to stay ➡ 20 ■ Where to eat ➡ 52 ➡ 54 ■ After dark ➡ 86 ➡ 90 ■ What to see ➡ 104 ➡ 118

Where to shop

John Lobb (34)
90 Jermyn Street, SW1 ☎ 0171-930 8089 ➡ 0171-839 0981

🔵 Green Park, Piccadilly Circus **Shoes, leather goods** 🕐 Mon.–Wed., Fri., Sat. 10am–6pm; Thur. 10am–7pm 🔲 💷 9 St James's Street, SW1 ☎ 0171-930 3664 (for made-to-measure items)

John Lobb is one of the finest makers of classic men's shoes in the world. This store offers the Lobb name, with ready-to-wear shoes costing from £250. For a made-to-measure pair expect to pay from £1,200 and a delivery time of up to six months.

Harvie & Hudson (35)
77 Jermyn Street, SW1 ☎ 0171-930 3949 ➡ 0171-839 7020

🔵 Green Park **Men's shirts** 🕐 Mon.–Sat. 9am–5.30pm 🔲 💷 97 Jermyn Street, SW1 ☎ 0171-839 3578; 55 Knightsbridge, SW1 ☎ 0171-235 2651

Jermyn Street is world-famous for its shirt-makers. Harvie & Hudson is one of the finest practitioners and one of the most approachable of these stores. Their range of ready-to-wear shirts is staggering, but if you want the perfect fit of a bespoke shirt be prepared to pay upward of £120 (with a minimum order of four).

Paxton & Whitfield (36)
93 Jermyn Street, SW1 ☎ 0171-930 0259 ➡ 0171-321 0621

🔵 Piccadilly Circus **Cheese** 🕐 Mon. 9.30am–5.30pm; Tue.–Sat. 9am–5.30pm 🔲

Paxton & Whitfield's has supplied cheeses to the well-to-do of St James's and Mayfair for 200 years. Although British classics such as Stilton and Caerphilly are given prominence, the best cheeses of Europe can also be found displayed in this suitably old-fashioned store. Bread, ham, chutneys and other delicatessen goods are also on sale.

James Lock (37)
6 St James's Street, SW1 ☎ 0171-930 5849 ➡ 0171-976 1908

🔵 Green Park **Hats** 🕐 Mon.–Fri. 9am–5.30pm; Sat. 9.30am–4.30pm 🔲

Founded in 1676, this wonderfully old-fashioned hat-maker has been at this location since 1759 and counts Nelson and Byron among its past customers. Almost any type of headwear can be made to measure by the skilled hatters, or you can settle for a traditional trilby, bowler, deerstalker or panama from the off-the-peg range. Ladies' hats are also available as well as a repair service and advice on hat care from the solicitous staff.

Not forgetting

■ **Floris (38)** 89 Jermyn Street, SW1 ☎ 0171-930 2885 *Quality perfumes and toiletries for men and women since the 1730s.* ■ **Turnbull & Asser (39)** 71–72 Jermyn Street, SW1 ☎ 0171-930 0502 *Top-quality made-to-measure shirts.* ■ **Berry Bros & Rudd (40)** 3 St James's Street, SW1 ☎ 0171-396 9600 *Highly respected and long established wine merchant.*

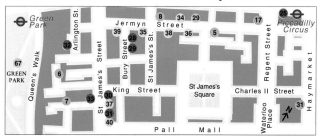

Green Park
Arlington St.
Jermyn Street
8 34 29
17
25 Piccadilly Circus
39
35
28
29
32
St James's Street
Bury Street
St James's St.
5
67 GREEN PARK
Queen's Walk
6
Regent Street
Haymarket
7
33
30
37
31
31
40
King Street
St James's Square
St James's Street
Charles II Street
Waterloo Place
31
Pall Mall

35

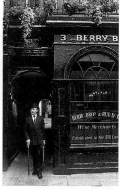

40

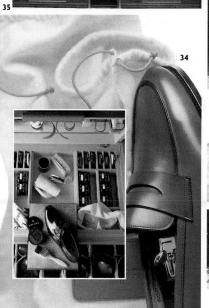

34

36

36

37

35

149

The name Piccadilly derives from 'picadil', a type of 17th-century collar, and quality clothing is still a specialty of this area. Situated between St James's and Mayfair and close to Buckingham Palace it is no surprise to find an abundance of stores boasting Royal warrants, as well as

Where to shop

Gieves & Hawkes (41)
1 Savile Row, W1 ☎ 0171-434 2001 ➡ 0171-437 1092

θ *Piccadilly Circus* **Gentlemen's tailor** ⊙ *Mon.–Wed., Fri., Sat. 9am–6pm; Thur. 9am–7pm* ▣ ◄► *18 Lime Street, EC3* ☎ *0171-283 4914*

Perhaps the most famous of the Savile Row tailors, Gieves & Hawkes started as a supplier of naval and military uniforms (the Duke of Wellington was a customer). Today, traditional styling and high-quality materials are still important, but there is more emphasis on off-the-peg ranges and the selection of shirts, jumpers, ties and other accessories.

Ozwald Boateng (42)
9 Vigo Street, W1 ☎ 0171-734 6868 ➡ 0171-734 3737

θ *Piccadilly Circus* **Gentlemen's tailor** ⊙ *Mon.–Sat. 10am–6pm* ▣

Ozwald Boateng's wonderful suits are as seriously stylish and daring as any you will find in London. Yet despite the rich and sometimes startling colors and fabrics he uses, these designs are definitely made to be worn. Ready-to-wear suits cost around around £600 while a bespoke version will cost upward of £1,300. The vibrant decor of the store is as flamboyant as the clothes and no doubt causes a few raised eyebrows from the traditionalist tailors of nearby Savile Row.

Penhaligon's (43)
16 Burlington Arcade, W1 ☎ 0171-629 1416 ➡ 0171-491 7536

θ *Green Park, Piccadilly Circus* **Perfumes** ⊙ *Mon.–Sat. 9.30am–5.30pm* ▣ ◄► *41 Wellington Street, WC2* ☎ *0171-836 2150; 20a Brooke Street, W1* ☎ *0171-493 0002; 8 Royal Exchange, Cornhill, EC3* ☎ *0171-283 0711*

Penhaligon's has been selling beautifully bottled, hand-blended perfumes since 1870 and many still follow the original recipes of the founder, William Henry Penhaligon. Prince Charles and the Duke of Edinburgh have bought their Lords, English Fern or Hannam Bouquet cologne here. Ladies, meanwhile, can choose from nostalgic scents such as Victorian Posy, Bluebell and Lily of the Valley.

Fortnum & Mason (44)
181 Piccadilly, W1 ☎ 0171-734 8040 ➡ 0171-437 3278

θ *Green Park* **Fine foods** ⊙ *Mon.–Sat. 9.30am–6pm* ▣

This company is nearly 300 years old and, although it is a department store, pride of place goes to the splendid food hall. Red carpets, glittering chandeliers and dark wood provide the setting for a fine range of fresh and packaged produce with an emphasis on teas, pies, biscuits and classic recipe chutneys and marmalades.

Not forgetting

■ **Irish Linen Co. (45)** 35–36 Burlington Arcade, W1 ☎ 0171-493 8949 *High-quality linen direct from Ireland.* ■ **Hatchards (46)** 187 Piccadilly, W1 ☎ 0171-439 9921 *Booksellers to the Queen, founded in 1797.*

several luxurious regal arcades in the Piccadilly area. ■ What to see ➥ 104

GIEVES & HAWKES
No.1 Savile Row, London

Where to shop

Electrum (47)
21 South Molton Street, W1 ☎ 0171-629 6325

🔵 *Bond Street* **Jewelry** 🕐 *Mon.–Fri. 10am–6pm; Sat. 10am–1pm* ▢

Some of the most inventive and stylish (if expensive) contemporary jewelry. More than 80 of top British and European jewelry designers are represented. Popular pieces include Mike Abbott and Kim Ellwood's wacky animal earrings and pins, and John Dennis's bold, chunky rings.

Gray's Antique Market (48)
South Molton Lane, W1 ☎ 0171-629 7034

🔵 *Bond Street* **Antiques** 🕐 *Mon.–Fri. 10am–6pm* ▢ *depending on the stall* ▢

A huge range of antiques can be found in this former Victorian plumbing factory and the nearby mews: ancient occidental and oriental artifacts, militaria and jewelry at fairly reasonable prices.

Vivienne Westwood (49)
6 Davies Street, W1 ☎ 0171-629 3757 ➡ 0171-629 3757

🔵 *Bond Street* **Women's ready-to-wear** 🕐 *Mon.–Wed., Fri., Sat. 10am–6pm; Thur. 10am–7pm* ▢ 🏢 *430 King's Road, SW3 ☎ 0171-352 6551; 44 Conduit Street, W1 ☎ 0171-439 1109*

Ever since her formative role in shaping the look of punk in the late 1970s, outrageous designs, bold colors and tartans have been Westwood's trademarks. This store stocks all her main men's and women's labels while the Davies Street outlet is home to the 'Gold' label and made-to-order service. Street-style clothes can be found at the King's Road store.

Charbonnel & Walker (50)
28 Old Bond Street, 1 Royal Arcade, W1
☎ 0171-491 0939 ➡ 0171-495 6279

🔵 *Green Park* **Chocolates** 🕐 *Mon.–Fri. 9am–6pm; Sat. 10am–5pm* ▢

This British company have been making superb hand-made chocolates and candies for over a century. Champagne truffles are a specialty and the violet creams are said to be a favorite of the Queen Mother.

G.F. Trumper (51)
9 Curzon Street, W1 ☎ 0171-499 1850 ➡ 0171-491 4924

🔵 *Green Park* **Barber** 🕐 *Mon.–Fri. 9am–5.30pm; Sat. 9am–1pm* ▢ 🏢 *20 Jermyn Street, SW1 ☎ 0171-734 1370*

Probably the most traditional of all London's barbers. Customers are seated in their own mahogany cubicle and treated to skilled haircuts and unsurpassable wet shaves by scrupulously polite waistcoated staff.

Not forgetting
■ **Mulberry (52)** 11–12 Gees Court, St Christopher's Place, W1 ☎ 0171-493 2546 *High-class purses, accessories and clothes.*

eat ➡ 54 ➡ 56 ➡ 58 ■ After dark ➡ 84 ➡ 92 ■ What to see ➡ 118 ■ Where to shop ➡ 138

50

51

47

50

51

51

Knightsbridge has always been an exclusive shopping area and it retains an upmarket atmosphere. Two well-known department stores are located here and the boutiques on Sloane Street are a who's-who of haute couture. ■ Where to stay ➡ 28 ➡ 30 ■ Where to eat ➡ 60

Where to shop

Harrods (1)
87–135 Brompton Road, SW1 ☎ 0171-730 1234 ➡ 0171-581 0470

⊖ Knightsbridge ◷ Mon.–Tue., Sat. 10am–6pm; Wed., Fri. 10am–7pm ▱

The scale of Harrods and the range of goods on offer is dizzying. Among the highlights are the elegant Egyptian hall and the cuddly toy department (featuring a life-size grizzly bear) but pride of place goes to the beautifully decorated food hall. Consisting of 18 departments spread over 35,000 square feet, it displays a stupendous selection of produce from all over the world.

Harvey Nichols (2)
109–125 Knightsbridge, SW1 ☎ 0171-235 5000 ➡ 0171-259 6084

⊖ Knightsbridge ◷ Mon., Tue., Thur., Fri. 10am–7pm; Sat. 10am–6pm; Sun. noon–5pm ▱ ⊞ Fifth Floor ➡ 60, The Foundation

While the tourists flock to Harrods, its smaller neighbor draws the fashion-conscious shoppers of Knightsbridge. Nowhere in London offers a better or wider selection of fashion labels. Ozbek, John Galliano, Dolce & Gabbana, Ralph Lauren, Armani and Dries Van Noten are just a few of the big names available. Harvey Nics (as it is informally known) is also notable for its superb window displays, its fine food hall and classy restaurant, The Fifth Floor ➡ 60.

Rigby & Peller (53)
2 Hans Road, SW3 ☎ 0171-589 9293 ➡ 0171-581 8915

⊖ Knightsbridge *Lingerie* ◷ Mon., Tue., Thur., Fri. 9am–6pm; Wed. 9am–7pm, Sat. 9.30am–6pm ▱ ⟨⟩ 22a Conduit Street, W1 ☎ 0171-491 2200

Exemplary service is the trademark of this corsetières, in business since 1939, and famed for supplying the Queen with her underwear. Big name and lesser-known lingerie brands are stocked plus a range of swimwear and nightclothes. Styles range from the regal to the racy.

The Conran Shop (54)
Michelin House, 81 Fulham Road, SW3
☎ 0171-589 7401 ➡ 0171-823 7015

⊖ South Kensington *Designer household goods* ◷ Mon., Thur., Fri. 9.30am– 6pm; Tue. 10am–6pm; Wed. 9.30am–7pm; Sat. 10am–6.30pm; Sun. noon–5.30pm ▱

No one has done more to revolutionize British design than Sir Terence Conran. His furniture and accessories store is worth a visit if only to see the wonderful art nouveau Michelin building in which it is housed. As might be expected, the emphasis is on classic, simple designs whether it is for a bottle opener, a pair of sunglasses, a watch or a piece of luggage. Plenty of gift ideas.

Not forgetting
■ **Katharine Hamnett (55)** 20 Sloane Street, SW1 ☎ 0171-823 1002 *Environmentally-aware cutting-edge fashion for men and women.*

➡ 62
■ What to
see ➡ 114 ➡
118

Kensington Road

HYDE PARK 68

The Carriage Road

Knightsbridge

Trevor Place

Kensington Road

Montpelier St.

Cheval Place

VICTORIA
& ALBERT
MUSEUM
55

Brompton Road

Cromwell Road

Thurloe
Square

Pelham Street

Egerton Gdns

Beauchamp Pl.

Ovington Sq.

Walton Street

Draycott Ave.

Sloane Ave.

Knightsbridge

Brompton Road

Hans Rd

53

28

Sloane Street

Lennox Gardens

Milner Street

25
26
27
61
55
1
Basil St.

Hans
Place

Pont Street

31

Cadogan
Square

55 54
54

Pavilion Road

Sloane Street

Lowndes Sq.

Hans Place

Pavilion Road

Cadogan Place

N

1

54

2

54

THE
CONRAN
SHOP

MICHELIN

54

Where to shop

Hackett (56)
137 Sloane Street, SW1 ☎ **0171-730 3331** ➡ **0171-730 3525**

🔵 *Sloane Square* **Ready-to-wear for men, barber** 🕐 *Mon., Tue., Thur.–Sat. 9.30am–6pm; Wed. 9.30am–7pm* 🔲 🔵 *seven outlets throughout London*

Hackett appears to be a traditional men's outfitters, but there is rather more style and humor to be found in their ranges than in those of some of their competitors. Sober suits and top hats are available, but look out for the decadent Oscar-Wilde-style crimson velvet smoking jackets, canary-yellow braces, purple corduroy trousers and the stripy socks. A barber and a bespoke suit service can be found on the premises.

Patrick Cox (57)
8 Symons Street, SW1 ☎ **0171-730 6504** ➡ **0171-259 0117**

🔵 *Sloane Square* **Shoes** 🕐 *Mon., Tue., Thur.–Sat. 10am–6pm; Wed. 10am–7pm* 🔲 🔵 *Patrick Cox Wannabe, 129 Sloane Street, SW1* ☎ *0171-730 8886*

The award-winning Patrick Cox is one of the top names in shoe design. He has been successful in bringing his own sense of style and taste to a wide range of men's and women's shoes ranging from the classic to the crazy. His Wannabe loafer has proved so popular that it now has a separate store to itself, and a range of street clothing to complement it.

Antiquarius (58)
131–141 King's Road, SW3 ☎ **0171-351 5353**

🔵 *Sloane Square* **Antiques** 🕐 *Mon.–Sat. 10am–6pm* 🔲 *depending on stall* 🔳

Billing itself as 'London's most famous antiques market', the 120 dealers in this extensive enclosed market have something for everyone. Most are friendly and approachable and are happy to talk you through everything from jewelry, gold and silverware, antique rugs and watches to art deco ceramics, pipes, oil paintings, china and vintage luggage. The market's café provides refreshment for tired antiques-hunters.

Heal's (59)
234 King's Road, SW3 ☎ **0171-349 8411** ➡ **0171-349 8439**

🔵 *Sloane Square* **Designer household goods** 🕐 *Mon.–Tue. 10am–6pm; Wed., Thur. 10am–7pm; Fri. 10am–6pm; Sun. noon–6pm* 🔲 🔵 *196 Tottenham Court Road, W1* ☎ *0171-636 1666*

Heal's has been a major name in the London design scene for more than 150 years, but this store only opened in the mid-1990s. Its trademark is selling clean, bright, bold designs at affordable prices. Among the most desirable items are chunky picture frames, tall bottles of designer cooking oils, colorful crockery and own-brand toiletries.

Not forgetting
■ **Henry Sotheran (60)** 80 Pimlico Road, SW1 ☎ 0171-730 8756 *Maps and prints.* ■ **Karen Millen (61)** 33 King's Road, SW3 ☎ 0171-730 7259 *Mid-range womenswear.* ■ **Steinberg & Tolkien (62)** 193 King's Road, SW3 ☎ 0171-376 3660 *Vintage clothes and jewelry.*

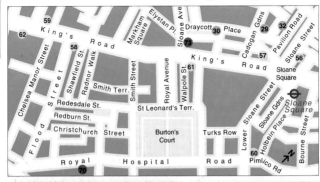

56

56

58

57

60

60

Nowhere else in London has the ethnic diversity, the mix of chic and shabby, and the vibrancy of Notting Hill. This is at its most striking around Portobello Road. Fruit stalls stand in front of antique dealers near to tattoo parlors next to accessory stores. ■ Where to stay ➡ 40

Where to shop

Books for Cooks (63)
4 Blenheim Crescent, W11 ☎ 0171-221 1992 ➡ 0171-221 1517

🟢 *Ladbroke Grove* **Cookbooks** 🕐 *Mon.–Sat. 9.30am–6pm* ▢ 🏠

Anyone with a passion for food and cooking will be in heaven in this tiny, overflowing bookstore. Knowledgeable, helpful staff will guide you to the secrets of Senegalese cuisine, treatises on the onion, macrobiotic cookbooks, histories of dining etiquette or any other specialty that interests you. Book ahead if you want to enjoy lunch at the equally minute café at the back of the shop where recipes from the books on sale are prepared freshly every day.

Graham & Green (64)
4, 7, 10 Elgin Crescent, W11 ☎ 0171-727 4594 ➡ 0171-229 9717

🟢 *Ladbroke Grove* **Designer household goods and gifts** 🕐 *Mon.–Fri. 10am–6pm; Sat. 9.30am–6pm; Sun. 11am–5pm* ▢ 🏠 *164 Regent's Park Road, NW1* ☎ *0171-586 2960*

These three small stores in one street sell faultlessly tasteful clothes, household goods, decorative items and gifts. No. 10 is where you'll find top womenswear designers such as Ghost, John Rocha and Comme Des Garçons. Lighthearted home accessories are the specialty of No. 7 with chunky Bodum pepper grinders, furry lampshades and wacky see-through inflatable chairs among the range of goods on display. Classic and ethnic housewares at No. 4 include Indian boxes, kilims, lamps, mirrors and beautifully made pyjamas and kimonos.

Aero (65)
96 Westbourne Grove, W2 ☎ 0171-221 1950 ➡ 0171-221 2555

🟢 *Bayswater, Notting Hill Gate* **Designer household goods** 🕐 *Mon.–Fri. 10am–6.30pm; Sat. 10am–6pm; Sun. noon–5pm* ▢

The British tend to be nervous of modern design and Aero is one of the few stores in London committed to changing this attitude by promoting the work of the best British and European contemporary designers. Elegant furniture, lighting and imaginative storage systems are housed in the basement, while the first floor is devoted to desirable accessories and household goods. Aero proves that even such mundane objects as wastebins can be objects of beauty.

Not forgetting

■ **The Body Shop (66)** 194 Portobello Road, W11 ☎ 0171-229 3928 *Environmentally-friendly cosmetics and toiletries chain with more than 25 outlets in London alone. The extraordinary success of its products has helped promote a fashion for eco-friendly, cruelty-free products made using natural ingredients.*
■ **Travel Bookshop (67)** 13 Blenheim Crescent, W11 ☎ 0171-229 5260 *Excellent selection of guidebooks and travel writing.*
■ **Wild at Heart (68)** 222 Westbourne Grove, Turquoise Island, W11 ☎ 0171-727 3095 *Flower store located within a striking modern public toilet.*

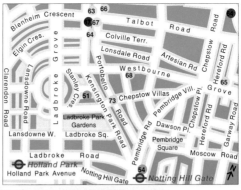

Blenheim Crescent
Elgin Cres.
Talbot Road
Colville Terr.
Lonsdale Road
Artesian Rd
Chepstow Road
Hereford Rd
Westbourne
Clarendon Road
Lansdowne Road
Ladbroke Grove
Stanley Cres.
Portobello Road
Kensington Park Road
68
Grove
63 66
67
64
65
63

73 Chepstow Villas
51
Ladbroke Park Gardens
Pembridge Vill.
Pembridge Pl.
Hereford Rd
Garway Road
Lansdowne W. Ladbroke Sq.
Dawson Pl.
Ladbroke Road
Pembridge Square
Moscow Road
Holland Park
54
Notting Hill Gate
Holland Park Avenue
Notting Hill Gate

The trend for ecologically friendly toiletries and cosmetics is largely attributable to the Body Shop.

Basic facts

London has a long tradition of street trading and there are more than a hundred markets throughout the capital offering everything from exotic fruit to rare antiques. Some – such as the massive Camden and Greenwich weekend markets – are aimed as much at visitors as

Where to shop

Camden (69)

⊖ Camden Town
🕓 Thur.–Sun.
9.30am–5pm
Camden Lock
(Camden Lock
Place) Sat.–Sun.
10am–6pm
**Stables, Camden
Canal market**
(Chalk Farm Road)
Sat.–Sun.
8am–6pm
Electric market
(Camden High
Street) Sun.
9am–5pm

Ever-expanding
and ever-popular,
Camden's endless
stalls of youth-
oriented new and
second-hand
clothes, Third
World crafts and
international food
are a major tourist
draw.

Columbia Road (70)

⊖ Old Street,
Bethnal Green
🕓 Sun. 8am–1pm

This East London
flower market
sells the most
wonderful array
of flowers, plants,
shrubs, containers
and other garden
delights to be
found in the
capital. Make sure
you arrive early if
you wish to avoid
the crush; and
arrive late if you
want to pick up
some extra-
ordinary bargains.

Brick Lane (71)

⊖ Liverpool Street,
Aldgate East, Old
Street, Shoreditch
🕓 Sun. 6am–1pm

There are all
manner of goods
on sale at this
impressive market,
from leather
goods, antiques
and car radios
through to
chocolates and
cheeses – you
name it, you will
probably find it
here, at this most
enjoyable and lively
of all London's
East End markets.
Why not try a
local specialty –
jellied eels (£1 per
portion) – from
one of the fish and
seafood stalls.

Spitalfields (72)

⊖ Liverpool Street
🕓 **General
market**
Mon.–Fri.
11am–3pm; Sun.
9am–3pm
**Organic
products**
Fri. 11am–3pm;
Sun. 9am–3pm

This market is at
its most interesting
on Sundays when
stalls selling
organic food and
crafts fill this huge,
hangar-like hall.
Antiques are
sold here on
Saturdays and
there is a general
market throughout
the rest of the
week.

residents while others – Brixton and Berwick Street, for example – remain authentic working markets.

Portobello Road (73)

🚇 Notting Hill Gate, Ladbroke Grove
🕐 **Bric-à-brac**
Fri. 7am–4pm; Sat. 7am–6pm; Sun. 9am–4pm
General market
Mon.–Wed. 9am–5pm; Thur. 9am–1pm; Fri.–Sat. 7am–6pm
Organic products
Thur. 11am–6pm
Fashionable Notting Hill's daily food market is supplemented by antique sellers and hip clothes and bric-à-brac stalls at the weekend.

Berwick Street (74)

🚇 Leicester Square, Piccadilly Circus
🕐 Mon.–Sat. 9am–6pm
The only surviving fruit and vegetable street market in central London. Prices are low, the range of produce excellent and there are even stalls selling herbs and spices, fish, and cheese. Other stalls offer household items, flowers and leather goods.

Covent Garden (75)

🚇 Covent Garden
🕐 daily 9am–5pm
Jewelry and crafts are the specialties of the Apple market within the Plaza, while the Jubilee, nearer to the tube station, is best for antiques on Mondays and crafts at the weekend.

Bermondsey (76)

🚇 Borough, London Bridge
🕐 Fri. 5am–2pm
The best antiques market in the city, but you will need to arrive early to find the finest pieces; dealers will have snapped up most of the real bargains by 9am.

Brixton (77)

🚇 Brixton
🕐 Mon., Tue., Thur.–Sat. 8am–5pm; Wed. 8am–1pm
Vibrant, diverse and cheap – Brixton's huge, and very popular market is famous for its superb selection of Afro-Caribbean food.

Greenwich (78)

🚢 Greenwich Pier
🚌 122, 126
🕐 Sat., Sun. 9am–6pm

A sprawling, diverse weekend market, best visited on Sundays, when there are stalls selling organic foods, antiques, jewelry, second-hand clothes, books, records, crafts and a variety of ephemera. Extremely popular with tourists ➡ 126.

Beware!
Take care when crossing the streets in London.
The warning '*look left*' or '*look right*' is painted on
many of the streets, to remind you which direction
the traffic will be coming from.

 # Finding your way

Orientation
London is made up of 32 boroughs
divided into districts or areas. An
address often includes the name of
the area. Postal codes begin with the
letters N (north), S (south), E (east)
or W (west), and take Charing Cross
Station as their reference point. The
letter 'C' (eg 'EC2', or 'WC2') refer
to the City area.

10 Maps

Different types of streets

Crescent (crescent-shaped street)
Fields (former fields)
Gardens (former gardens)
Gate (former entrance)
Gore (wedge-shaped piece of land)
Lane (former laneway)
Place (usually a Square)
Row (street)
Street (usually smaller than a road)
Terrace (row of adjoined houses)
Villas (street lined with individual houses)
Walk (former path)

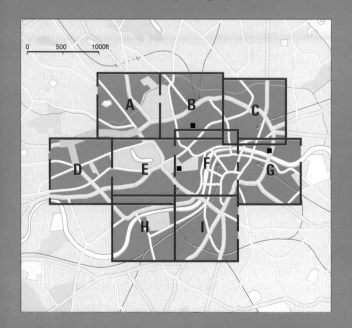

Street index

Each street mentioned is given a
map reference in bold (A, B, C, D, E,
F, G, H or I) followed by the actual
map co-ordinates for that street.

Index

Abbreviations

Ave. = Avenue	Rd = Road	St = Saint	Tube = Underground
Cres. = Crescent	Sq. = Square	Terr. = Terrace	station
Pl. = Place	St. = Street	Yd = Yard	

Tube map

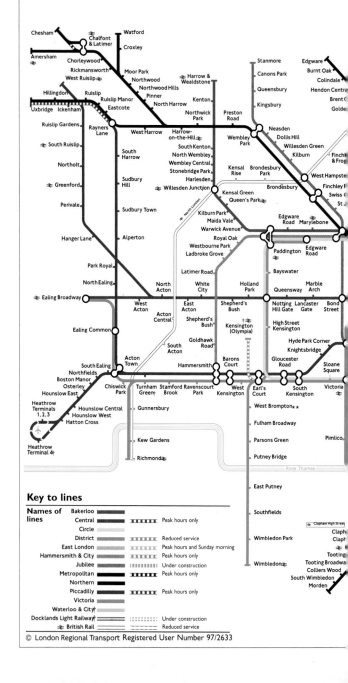

UNDERGROUND

Passenger information
☎ 0171-222 1234
London Travel Check
☎ 0171-222 1200

High Barnet
Totteridge & Whetstone
Mill Hill East
Woodside Park
West Finchley
Finchley Central
East Finchley
Highgate
Archway
Tufnell Park

Cockfosters
Oakwood
Southgate
Arnos Grove
Bounds Green
Wood Green
Turnpike Lane
Manor House

Tottenham Hale
Seven Sisters
Blackhorse Road
Walthamstow Central

Hampstead Heath
Gospel Oak
Kentish Town West
Chalk Farm
Camden Town
Mornington Crescent

Kentish Town
Camden Road
North London

Arsenal
Holloway Road
Caledonian Road
Drayton Park ★★ †

Finsbury Park

King's Cross St Pancras
Euston
Angel

Caledonian Road & Barnsbury
Highbury & Islington
Canonbury
Hackney Central
Hackney Wick
Homerton
North Woolwich

Essex Road † ★★
Dalston Kingsland

ren Street
Euston Square
Euston
Goodge Street
Russell Square
Thameslink
Holborn
Farringdon
Barbican †
Moorgate

Old Street
Liverpool Street
Bethnal Green
Mile End
Epping Hainault
Upminster

Shoreditch
Stepney Green
Whitechapel

ottenham Court Road
Chancery Lane ★
Covent Garden
Leicester Square ★★ City Thameslink
St Paul's
Cannon Street
Bank
Aldgate East
Aldgate

Westferry
Beckton Island Gardens

adilly ircus
Charing Cross
Blackfriars ★Temple
Mansion House
Monument Tower Hill
Fenchurch Street
Shadwell
Limehouse

stminster
Embankment
River Thames

Tower Gateway
Wapping

Canary Wharf

Rotherhithe

Waterloo
Southwark
London Bridge
Under construction

Bermondsey
Canada Water
Surrey Quays

Lambeth North
Borough

New Cross Gate
New Cross

l ⇌
Elephant & Castle ♿

Kennington
Oval
Brixton ♿

○ Interchange stations
⇌ Connections with British Rail
⇌ Connections with British Rail within walking distance

✝ Airport interchange
★ Closed Sundays
★★ Closed Saturdays and Sundays

◊ Mornington Crescent closed for rebuilding

† Opening times are displayed in each station
(some stations are closed on public holidays)

Diary 1B 4. 96

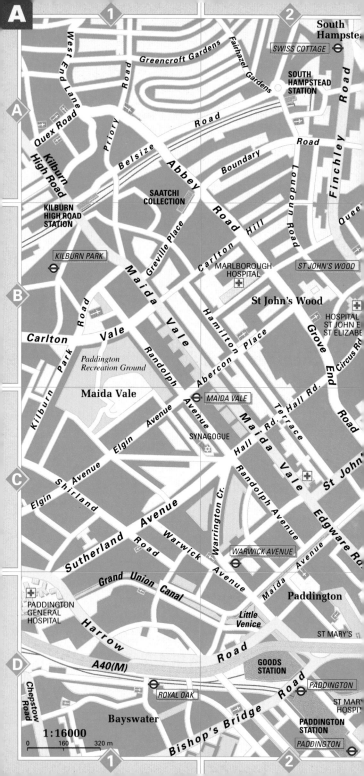

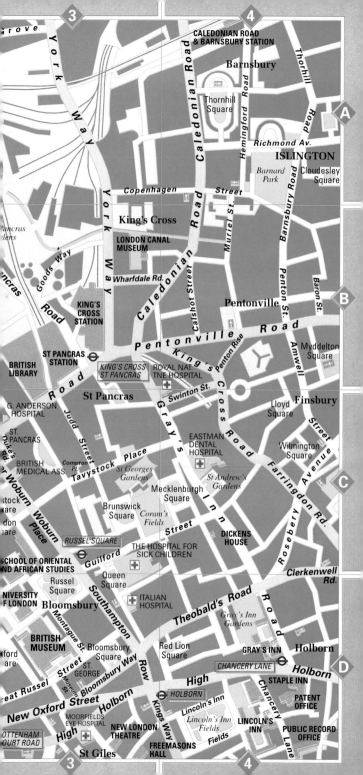

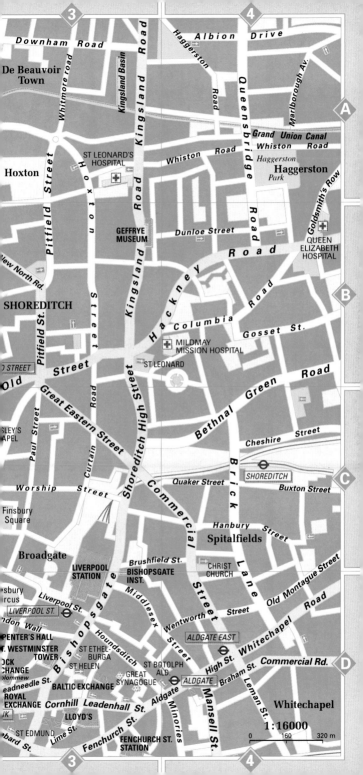

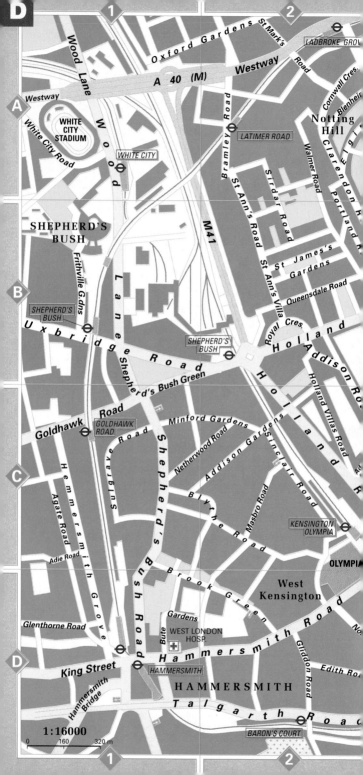

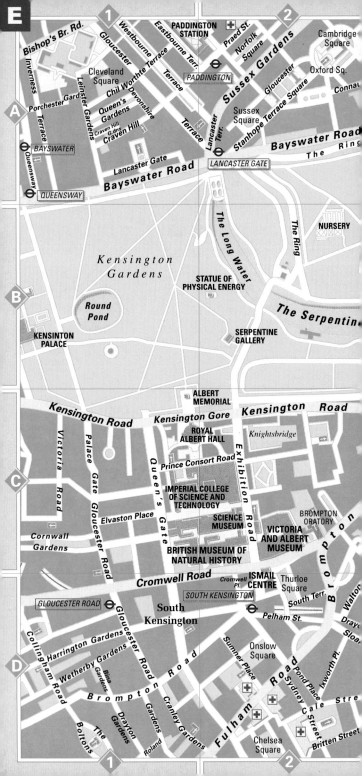

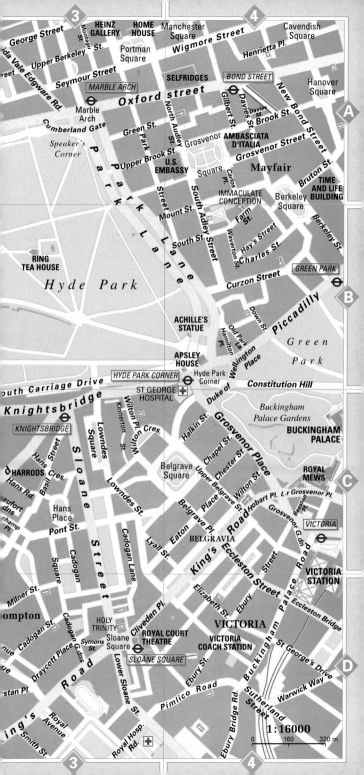

F

ALL SOULS CHURCH

ST GEORGE

POLYTECHNIC INST.

ST PATRICK

New Oxford S

High Holborn

Cavendish Square

OXFORD CIRCUS

Oxford Street

Soho

TOTTENHAM COURT ROAD

ST GILES

St Giles High St.

High Holborn

Sho
G.C.
RO
OP
HO

St Gile

A

Hanover Square

Newman St.

Soho Square

Greek St.

Charing Cross

St Giles

Neal's Yd.

Earlham St.

RO
OP
HO

COVENT GARDE

Regent Street

Argyll St.

Great Marlborough St.

Berwick Street

Wardour Street

Dean Street

Frith St.

Old Compton St.

Shaftesbury Avenue

Monmouth St.

Long Acre

Floral St.

King S

St George St.

Conduit St.

Kingly St.

Savile Row

Marshall St.

Broadwick St.

Lexington St.

Rupert St.

Newport Pl.

Garrard St.

St. Newport St.

Great Newport St.

LEICESTER SQ.

Shelton

Beak St.

Brewer St.

Lisle St.

Cranbourn St.

Floral St.

TIME AND LIFE BUILDING

Berkeley St.

Old Bond St.

Albemarle St.

Dover St.

The Quadrant

Vigo St.

BURLINGTON HOUSE

Piccadilly Circus

Coventry St.

LONDON PAVILION

Haymarket

Regent Street

Whitcomb St.

Panton St.

DESIGN CENTRE

NATIONAL GALLERY

CHARING CROSS HOSP.

William IV St.

Str

Villiers

Burlington Arc.

B

Piccadilly

Jermyn St.

Bury St.

King St.

St James's

St James's Square

ROYAL OPERA ARC.

Pall Mall East

Cockspur St.

Trafalgar Square

Northumberland

CHARING CROS

Queen's Walk

Arlington St.

St James's St.

Pall Mall

Waterloo Pl.

ADMIRALTY ARCH

OLD ADMIRALTY

Whitehall

Whitehall Pl.

OLD W
OFFICE

Green Park

ST JAMES'S PALACE

LANCASTER HOUSE

St James's MARLBOROUGH HOUSE

The Mall

St James's Park

Horse Guards Road

HORSE GUARDS

TREASURY

Parliament St.

BANQUE
HOUSE

QUEEN VICTORIA MEMORIAL

GOVERNMENT OFFICES

King Charles St.

WESTMINSTER

Costitution Hill

BUCKINGHAM PALACE

Birdcage Walk

Great George St.

Bridge S

C

ROYAL MEWS

Buckingham Gate

M. GUILDHALL

METHODIST CENTRAL HALL

Tothill St.

Parliament Square

BIG BEN

HOUSES
PARLIAME

Old Palace Yard

Bressenden Pl.

Buckingham Palace Road

WELLINGTON BARRACKS

Palace Street

Petty France

NEW SCOTLAND YARD

ST JAMES'S PARK

BOARD OF TRADE

WESTMINSTER ABBEY

Dean's Yard

Great Smith St.

CHURCH HOUSE

Abingdon St.

VICTORIA

Victoria Street

WESTMINSTER CATHEDRAL

Great Peter Street

Marsham Street

WESTMINSTER

Smith Square

VICTORIA STATION

Witton Road

Vauxhall Bridge Road

Francis Street

Rochester Row

Vincent Square

Horseferry Road

Regency Street

Vincent St.

Istip St.

MILBANK TOWER

D

Belgrave Road

Eccleston St.

George's Drive

Warwick Square

Denbigh Road

Vincent Square

Vincent St.

John Istip St.

Millbank

TATE GALLERY

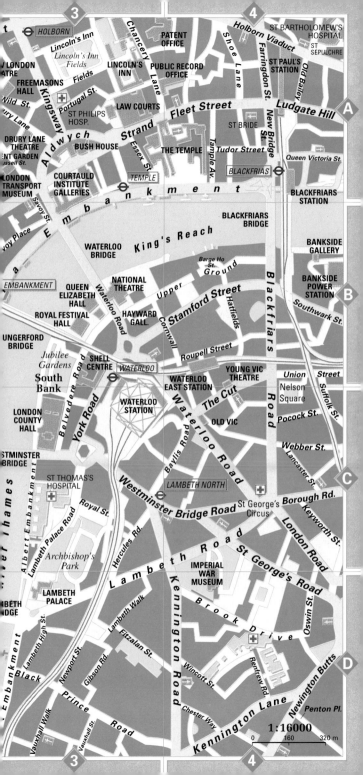

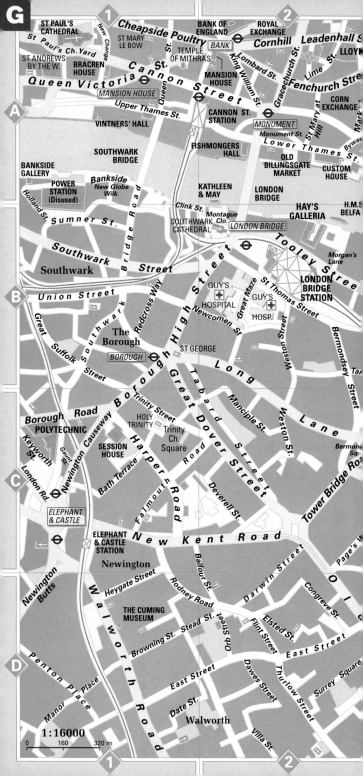

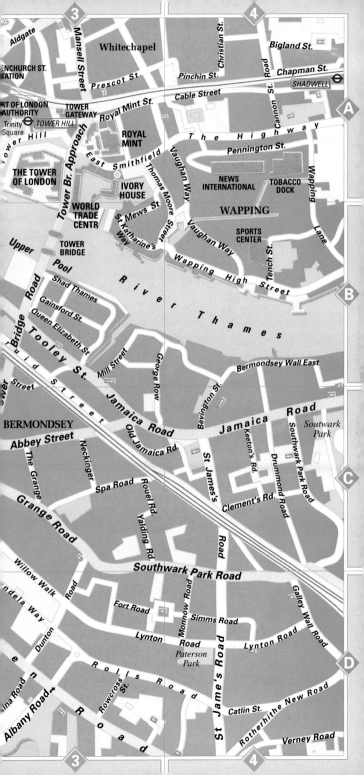

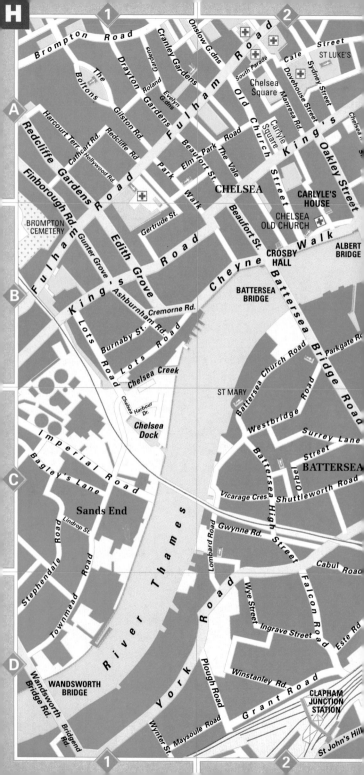

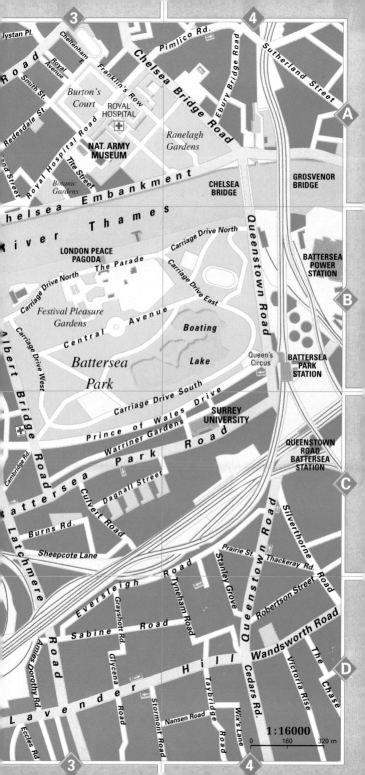

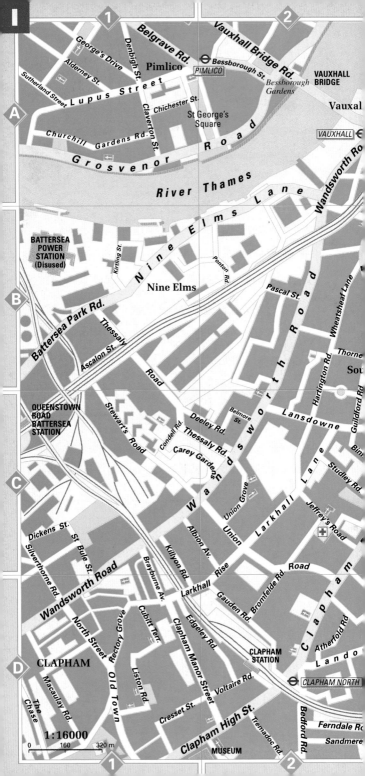

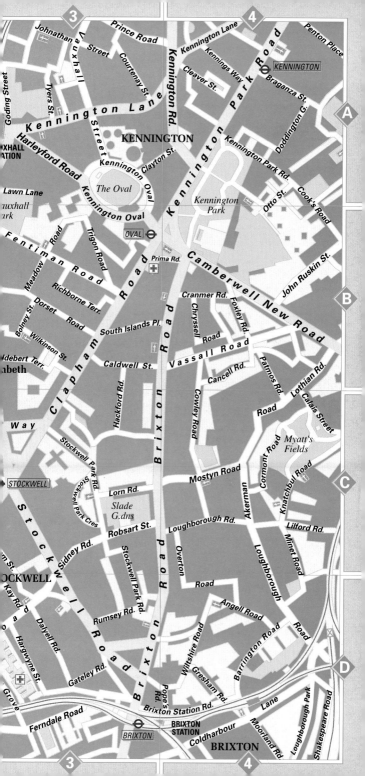

With thanks to the *British Tourist Authority* (Paris), the *London Tourist Board* (London) and all establishments mentioned in this guide, for their co-operation.

Picture
Credits